D0687106

THE INDIAN RENAISSANCE

THE INDIAN RENAISSANCE

India's Rise after a
Thousand Years of Decline

SANJEEV SANYAL

PENGUIN
VIKING

Library Resource Center
Renton Technical College
3000 N.E. 4th Street
Renton, WA 98056

VIKING

Published by the Penguin Group

Penguin Books India Pvt. Ltd, 11 Community Centre, Panchsheel Park, New Delhi 110 017, India

Penguin Group (USA) Inc., 375 Hudson Street, New York, New York 10014, USA

Penguin Group (Canada), 90 Eglinton Avenue East, Suite 700, Toronto, Ontario, M4P 2Y3, Canada (a division of Pearson Penguin Canada Inc.)

Penguin Books Ltd, 80 Strand, London WC2R 0RL, England

Penguin Ireland, 25 St Stephen's Green, Dublin 2, Ireland (a division of Penguin Books Ltd)

Penguin Group (Australia), 250 Camberwell Road, Camberwell, Victoria 3124, Australia (a division of Pearson Australia Group Pty Ltd)

Penguin Group (NZ), 67 Apollo Drive, Rosedale, North Shore 0632, New Zealand (a division of Pearson New Zealand Ltd)

Penguin Group (South Africa) (Pty) Ltd, 24 Sturdee Avenue, Rosebank, Johannesburg 2196, South Africa

Penguin Books Ltd, Registered Offices: 80 Strand, London WC2R 0RL, England

First published in Viking by Penguin Books India 2008

Copyright © Sanjeev Sanyal 2008

All rights reserved

10 9 8 7 6 5 4

ISBN   9780670082629

Typeset in Sabon Roman by SÜRYA, New Delhi
Printed at Chaman Offset Printers, New Delhi

330.954 SANYAL 2008

Sanyal, Sanjeev.

The Indian renaissance

This book is sold subject to the condition that it shall not, by way of trade or otherwise, be lent, resold, hired out, or otherwise circulated without the publisher's prior written consent in any form of binding or cover other than that in which it is published and without a similar condition including this condition being imposed on the subsequent purchaser and without limiting the rights under copyright reserved above, no part of this publication may be reproduced, stored in or introduced into a retrieval system, or transmitted in any form or by any means (electronic, mechanical, photocopying, recording or otherwise), without the prior written permission of both the copyright owner and the above-mentioned publisher of this book.

Contents

Acknowledgements   *vii*

1. Waiting for a Thousand Years   1

2. From Independence to Freedom   28

3. The Entrepreneurial Explosion   52

4. The Great Indian Middle Class and Its Limitations   80

5. Poverty, Inequality and the Last Bastion of Control   98

6. Two Revolutions   122

7. The Importance of Institutional Reform   147

8. How India Will Change   164

9. Is India's Rise Inevitable?   194

Notes   206
Index   219

Acknowledgements

There are many people without whom this book would never have been written and published. I would like to acknowledge with gratitude the debts I owe to friends, family and the staff at Penguin who helped me at various stages of the process.

Let me begin by thanking my editor Heather Adams whose sunny enthusiasm kept me going through the various drafts. I am also grateful to Manu Bhaskaran, Chapal Mehra, Krishan Chopra, Sandhya, Max Phua, Ravi Singh and Mimi Choudhury for their faith in my ideas. I would not have embarked on this project without their support.

A special thanks to Ramkishen Rajan, Shashi Tharoor, Amit Prakash, Vikram Khanna, Vijay Kelkar, Anupam Yog, Rajeev Suri, my brother Saurav and my father for reading through the drafts and providing many valuable comments.

Last, but not the least, I must thank my wife Smita for putting up with an anti-social author over eighteen months and for patiently reading and re-reading the chapters as they took shape.

Of course, I take full responsibility for any errors and omissions.

1

Waiting for a Thousand Years

When future generations of Indian school-children read history, they will be made to memorize two important dates from the twentieth century—1947 and 1991. The importance of the first is obvious. It was the year when India gained independence from Britain, a colonial power that had dominated the country since the eighteenth century.[1] Despite the bitterness of the sub-continent's partition into Muslim-majority Pakistan and Hindu-majority India, the year 1947 was undoubtedly an important turning point in the country's history.

What of 1991? It was the year that India decided to liberalize its economy, but can it be said to be a turning point comparable to 1947? For almost half a century, the country had been held down by self-imposed constraints that had hampered economic development and stunted its international stature. Liberalization has clearly unleashed the country's economic potential. However, the shift in 1991 was not just about changing economic policies but about gaining freedom from a cultural attitude embodied in the old inward-looking economic regime. The regime is usually associated with Jawaharlal Nehru, India's first Prime Minister, and his advisor Mahalanobis. However, the 'Nehruvian Vision' was only the latest manifestation of an inward-looking cultural attitude that had held down the Indian civilization for almost a millennium— far longer than foreign conquerors.

India has a long and proud history. However, during its 'golden age', prior to the eleventh century, it was a country that encouraged innovation and change. Indian society celebrated its risk-takers. It was open to foreign trade, ideas and immigrants. Foreign students flocked to its universities even as foreign merchants flocked to its ports. Yet a change in cultural attitudes by the eleventh century created a fossilized society obsessed with regulating all aspects of life according to fixed rules. Not surprisingly, this discouraged the spirit of innovation and led to a long and painful decline. India fell behind not just as an economy but as a civilization.

The year 1991 marks the turning point when India was forced to open itself out to the world. The 'opening' was not limited to the economy but to all aspects of life, and the process was sped up by the fact that it coincided with the communications revolution—cable television, mobile telephones, and the internet. This book argues that the long-term impact of this on India will be similar to what was witnessed in Western Europe following the Renaissance.

Of course, the process of change did not begin suddenly in 1991. It has its roots in early nineteenth-century Bengal. Thanks to Raja Ram Mohan Roy and his fellow reformers, the country witnessed important social reforms as well as the introduction of the English language. The process gradually spread through the country till the middle of the twentieth century. Independence from colonization should have accelerated the process but unfortunately it led to a reversion to isolationism. Instead of catching up with the world, the country fell even further behind.

It was only with the opening of India in the nineteen-nineties that the country has seen a renaissance both as an economy and as a civilization. The efforts of the nineteenth-century reformers had prepared India for the flood of ideas. Moreover, the country also now had a large and successful global diaspora that provided the country with international linkages that it had not enjoyed since the days of the ancient spice trade.[2] Within a few years, there was a major shift in India's cultural attitude to change. In this sense, the year 1991 has the same importance in Indian history as the Meiji Restoration had in Japanese history when instead of whining about the rest of the world, Indians began to believe in themselves again.

This book is about how India has finally become free, and how it has the opportunity now of transforming itself and the world. There are many hurdles on the way—the poor state of the institutions of governance, the quality of tertiary education and so on. However, there are also strong forces that will support India's transformation. Demographic change and a primary education revolution are unleashing the same dynamics that have already transformed the rest of Asia. A middle class is emerging that will soon demand major institutional and political change. India's rise is not predestined but, for the first time in a millennium, it looks like it has the courage to exploit the window of opportunity.

This book largely deals with India's economic resurgence. However, throughout the book, we will be mindful that economic resurgence is only part of a wider civilizational reawakening. An open cultural attitude is perhaps the single most important condition for an Indian renaissance—far more important and long lasting than demographic shifts and rising savings rates. Both the rise of Europe following the Renaissance and the revival of Japan after the Meiji Restoration predated their demographic shifts. Rising savings rates and literacy rates were important to the extent that they accelerated the pace at which new ideas and technologies were disseminated and absorbed. By themselves, labour and capital are not sufficient. The experience of the communist bloc during the course of the twentieth century clearly shows the limitations of generating growth by deploying capital and labour without an open cultural system. In the end, these societies simply could not deal with change despite their ability to generate complex new technologies. It is the same reason that the Nehru–Mahalanobis attempt to modernize India through the public sector was doomed to failure even if it had survived to see the demographic and literacy shifts.

These days it is commonplace to hear talk about how India is emerging as a great economic superpower and how, together with China, it is reshaping the world production system. The next two chapters look back at the sequence of events that brought India to this juncture. In subsequent chapters, we look at the emerging forces of demographic change, urbanization, growing middle-class and rising literacy levels. We also look at the major hurdles that India needs to cross and the risks that it must face. Finally, we will speculate on how India will change in the twenty-first century.

Before we go on to discuss India's present and its future, it is important to briefly look back at its past. Most people would think that India's decline began with European colonization in the eighteenth century. However, the country's relative international position had been in almost continuous decline for over a thousand years, predating not just the European colonization but even Mahmud Ghazni's infamous raids in the eleventh century. To understand the magnitude of the decline, we will look back at India's pre-eminent position in the world economy in ancient times. Only then can we fully appreciate the wider importance of the transformation India has experienced in the last decade and a half.

The 'Golden' Past

India was home to one of the earliest human civilizations. The Indus Valley Civilization (also called the Harappan civilization) flourished between 3300 and 2000 BC in what is now north-western India and Pakistan.[3] It was a contemporary of the ancient Chinese, Mesopotamian and Egyptian civilizations. Very little is known about the history of the civilization since few written records have been found and the script is yet to be deciphered. However, the ruins of its cities are extraordinary and suggest a very sophisticated economy that was able to support major urban centres.

Unlike its contemporary civilizations, the Harappans did not build grand buildings to rival the Egyptian pyramids. Instead, the Harrapan sites are more remarkable for their attention to urban planning. Their towns appear to be built around standardized plans that included plumbing, street-grids, granaries, public baths and other civic amenities. Most modern Indian towns would do well to emulate their example. It would not be unreasonable to say that the average Indian of that era would have enjoyed a standard of living that was far higher than that of his/her contemporaries in other parts of the world.

Most interestingly for our current purposes, there is strong evidence that the Indus Valley had active trade links with the outside world, particularly Mesopotamia. Archaeologists have uncovered a sophisticated system of docks for sea-going vessels in the port city of Lothal in Gujarat. Some historians link it to a land the ancient Sumerians called 'Meluhha'. It is unclear what these Bronze Age civilizations traded, but Mesopotamian sites have yielded many terracotta seals from the Indus Valley. These seals were likely to have been used by merchants to mark individual shipments.

The Indus Valley Civilization eventually went into decline around 1800 BC. It is not known why it declined. The old 'Aryan Invasion Theory' is now largely discredited and the currently fashionable view is that it had something to do with desertification and other environmental changes. The archaeological and cultural evidence shows that the focus now shifted further east to the Gangetic plains. It was here, in the fourth century BC, that the Mauryan empire rose. According to tradition, the Mauryan empire was built by Chanakya (also called Kautilya), a professor of Political Economy at Takshila University.[4] Together with his pupil Chandragupta Maurya, he created the Mauryan empire in order to check the advance of the Macedonian Greeks led by Alexander. The two built the largest political entity India has ever seen, covering virtually all of the Indian subcontinent and with its capital in Pataliputra (near modern Patna). In 305 BC, Chandragupta defeated the Macedonian general Seleucus Nikator, Alexander's successor in Asia, to secure Afghanistan and possibly parts of eastern Iran.

What we know about the Mauryan empire suggests a very prosperous country with an efficiently run administration. Foreign trade flourished and was officially encouraged. We can deduce this from Kautilya's *Arthashastra*, a treatise on public administration and political economy, that was possibly meant as a manual for the running of the newly established empire. It clearly highlights the importance of foreign trade both by land and by sea. The *Arthashastra* calls for the appointment of senior officials to look after highways and ports as well as to encourage foreign trade. Kautilya specifically recommended that when it is inefficient to produce certain goods locally, officials should keep in mind the advantages of importing goods from another country.[5] It is amazing that, twenty-three centuries ago, Kautilya was explicitly thinking about comparative advantage and the international division of labour!

In his book *Indika*, Greek ambassador Megasthenes[6] described a country with a well-irrigated agricultural system and a sophisticated artisan manufacturing sector. It is clear that India's economy was considered very advanced at that time. This does not mean that Indians were too proud to absorb new ideas from the Greeks. In subsequent centuries, Greeks influence was clearly visible in areas ranging from sculpture to coinage. Even the Hindu temple may be of Greek origin. The ancient Vedic texts suggest that Hindus originally did not worship idols and build temples, and it is quite likely that both Hindus and Buddhists got the idea from the Greeks.

Many kingdoms rose and fell during the centuries that followed the decline of the Mauryan empire but India remained a major economic power. According to Angus Maddison's estimates, India accounted for 33 per cent of the world economy in AD 1.[7] India's share was three times the share of Western Europe and was much larger than that of Roman Empire as a whole (21.5 per cent). China's share was 26 per cent of world GDP and was significantly less than that of India. In other words, India was by far the world's economic superpower at that time.

Over the centuries, economic activity in the coastal areas of the southern peninsula grew to rival that of the northern plains. This may be partly due to the disruptions caused in the north-west by periodic invasions by Central Asian tribes. However, the shift was encouraged by a boom in maritime trade. There is evidence that by first century BC India was at the centre of a complex maritime trade network functioning in the Indian Ocean. This boom in maritime trade was made possible by the discovery of the regular directional shifts in the monsoon winds, a discovery that Greek sources credit to the navigator Hippalus. As a result, a number of major ports appeared on both coasts such as Tamralipti (modern Tamluk in Bengal) and Muzaris (usually identified as Kodungallur in Kerala).

To the east, the Indian Ocean maritime network extended as far as the Hindu kingdom of Champa (in modern-day Vietnam) where Indian merchants must have exchanged goods with Chinese merchants. There are also numerous references in Indian sources to the islands of Yavadwipa and Suwarnadwipa, usually identified with Java and Sumatra respectively. India exported textiles, metalware and pepper in exchange for spices and gold. Other than black pepper, most of the spices that Europeans then thought of as Indian spices actually came from Indonesian islands where they had been purchased by Indian merchants. The beautifully carved panels of Borobodur in central Java show goods-laden merchant ships that criss-crossed the Indian Ocean.

In the popular imagination, the Silk Route through Central Asia is usually regarded as the arterial highway of ancient East–West trade. The romantic image of the Silk Route owes much to the writings of Marco Polo. However, it is more likely that the southern 'Spice Route' was the more important trade route between the Mediterranean world and Asia. Even Marco Polo returned home to Italy by the southern sea route and has left interesting accounts of his journey through South-East Asia and the southern Indian coast.

The cultural impact of this era on South-east Asia remains clearly visible. It may be most obvious in the Hindu island of Bali, the ruins of Angkor and in Buddhist Thailand but, throughout the region, the influence of ancient India is evident in everyday life, from personal names to the immense popularity of the epic *Ramayana*. The national languages of both Malaysia and Indonesia is 'Bahasa' which is full of words derived from Sanskrit. Indeed the name 'Bahasa' itself is derived from the Sanskrit word 'bhasha', meaning language. To this day, the coronation of the king of Thailand and other royal ceremonies are carried out by Hindu Brahmin priests.

In India too, cultural traditions continue to recall these ancient trade routes. For instance, in the state of Orissa, the festival of Kartik Purnima still celebrates the day on which the Sadhaba merchants set sail for far-off lands. A large fair called 'Bali-yatra' is held in the town in Cuttack which scholars think marks the annual departure of merchant fleets for the island of Bali.[8] The voyages to South-east Asia were long and dangerous. These festivals echo a culture that celebrated its entrepreneurs and risk-takers.

India's maritime links extended to the west as well where it traded with the Persian and Roman empires. There were two main routes—one via the Red Sea and one through the Persian Gulf. From there, they made their way in caravans through the desert (and/or sailed up the Nile) to Mediterranean ports such as Alexandria. Indians sold textiles, spices (some that they had brought from South-east Asia) and other luxuries. Black pepper from the Malabar was a particularly important export and it was sold in such large quantities that it was widely available even as far away as Roman-controlled Britain.

Interestingly, the most important items that the Indians seem to have demanded in payment from the West were precious metals. Thus, the Indian trade surplus with the Roman Empire caused a constant one-way flow of gold coins. Roman writer Pliny (AD 23–79) wrote: 'Not a year passed in which India did not take fifty million sesterces away from

Rome.' The drainage of gold was a so serious that Emperor Vespasian was forced to discourage the imports of Indian luxury goods and ban the export of gold to India in the first century AD.[9] As a result of these centuries of trade surpluses, Indians accumulated a large store of gold. It is estimated that even today some 25–30 per cent of all the gold ever mined is held by Indian households in the form of jewellery even though the country itself has very few gold mines of its own.

The growth in maritime trade does not mean that the land routes in the north were abandoned. Despite periodic disruptions, trade routes through Central Asia (a branch of the Silk Route) continued to flourish though the first millennium. Note, however, that India's pre-eminent position was not limited to trade and economics alone. Indian mathematicians, astronomers, metallurgists and physicians were arguably among the best in the world and were held is high regard.

The treatise on surgery by Sushruta (circa fifth century BC) describes a hundred and twenty surgical instruments and three hundred procedures. Plastic surgery was a routine procedure. Meanwhile, Indian mathematicians made extraordinary innovations, including the concept of zero, that is the basis of the numerical system that we use today. During the Gupta empire (third to fifth centuries AD), the astronomer-mathematician Aryabhatta was able to work out that the earth is spherical and that it rotates on its axis. He argued that the phases of the moon were due to the movement of shadows and that the planets shone through reflected light. He even made remarkably accurate estimates of the circumference of the earth and of the ratio pi. All this, a thousand years before Copernicus and Galileo.

Throughout these centuries India also produced remarkable works in art, literature and philosophy. Hindu–Buddhist kingdoms from South-east Asia to Central Asia looked to India for intellectual and cultural leadership. Pilgrims and students came by both land and sea routes to study in Indian universities like Taxila, Nalanda and Ujjaini and to visit the holy sites. Much of what we know about ancient India comes from the diaries of these foreign visitors. In common with the famous universities of today, the prestige of these ancient seats of learning attracted international endowments. An inscription dated AD 860 tells of how the king of Suwarnadvipa (Sumatra) made an endowment to Nalanda.

All in all, India had an extraordinary economic, intellectual and cultural influence throughout the ancient world. Moreover, this was an influence that was almost entirely exercised through peaceful means. With the one notable exception of the Chola naval raid on the Srivijaya kingdom in Sumatra in AD 1025, there are virtually no records of offensive Indian military intervention outside of the subcontinent.

In a way, India's place in the ancient world was similar to that which is occupied by the United States today. It was not only the dominant centre of economic and cultural activity but also a magnet for various groups of people who came to seek either fortune or refuge from persecution. Not many people realize that India is host to one of the oldest Jewish communities in the world. It is believed that the earliest Jews came to trade at the time of King Solomon but, after the destruction of the Second Temple by the Romans in AD 70, many refugees settled in Kerala. Some of their descendants still live in India. India is also host to the last remnants of the once powerful Zoroastrian tradition. They fled persecution in Iran in the eighth century and settled in Gujarat. Known as the Parsis, they are today a very successful business community. These are but a few examples of the numerous immigrant groups that settled in India during its golden age.

The picture of ancient India is of a society that encouraged

Renton Jech Coll Library

innovation and risk-taking. It was open to foreign trade, ideas, international students and political refugees. It is true that ancient texts sometimes refer to foreigners as 'mlecchas' or barbarians but this does not seem to have prevented the exchange of goods and ideas. If anything, this exchange was celebrated in festivals and folklore. Unfortunately, this open attitude did not last forever.

The Decline

India appears to have maintained its position as a pre-eminent economic and cultural world power till around the eleventh century. After this, its relative position steadily declined. It is striking that all of India's great contributions to the world were devised prior to the this date—yoga, algebra, the concept of zero, chess, plastic surgery, metallurgy, Hinduism, Buddhism and so on. Even the last great flowering of ancient Hindu culture was not in India itself but in the faraway empires of Angkor (Cambodia) and the Majapahit (Indonesia). In both these cases, the evidence clearly shows that cultural innovation was increasingly indigenously generated after the eleventh century rather than inspired by contemporary India.

Between AD 1000 and 1820, India's share of world GDP fell from 29 per cent to 16 per cent. In other words, India's position was in decline well before the colonial period. The Industrial Revolution and colonial occupation only sped up the process. As the Industrial Revolution spread through Europe and North America, India fell even further behind. When India gained independence in 1947, its share in world GDP was barely 4 per cent and this fell to 3 per cent by the time it liberalized its economy in 1991. Of course, India's economy did grow in absolute terms during this millennium but it fell far behind the rest of the world.

Contrast this with what happened in other parts of the world. China, and then Western Europe, bypassed India as the economic engines of the world. In AD 1000, China's economy was 23 per cent of the world economy (a bit more than three-fourth the size of the Indian economy). However, by 1500 it was the same size as India's and thereafter has always remained significantly larger. Western Europe went through an even larger relative shift. During the first millennium of the Common Era, following the collapse of the Roman Empire, the European economy went into decline in both relative and absolute terms. However, this changed dramatically as the Renaissance gradually took hold. Between 1000 and 1500, Western Europe's economy grew fourfold and its share in world GDP doubled, from 9 per cent to 18 per cent. Thereafter, its share rose at an accelerated pace. By 1820, as the Industrial Revolution was taking root, Western Europe accounted for almost a quarter of the world economy. Industrialization widened the gap further, especially if one includes the contributions of western offshoots such as the United States. Together with the United States and other offshoots, the West accounted for almost 60 per cent of the world's economic output by 1950.[10]

Of course sheer size is not the only indicator of relative economic progress but the trends in per capita income also tell a very similar story. According to Angus Maddison's estimates, India, China and Western Europe had roughly the same per capita income in AD 0.[11] Standards of living declined in Europe after the collapse of the Roman Empire and by AD 1000 we find that both China and India had average per capita incomes that were 113 per cent of Western European standards. However, the situation reversed as Europe went through the Renaissance and by AD 1500, India's per capita income was only 71 per cent of Western Europe's while China's was at 78 per cent.

From here European powers began to dominate the world.

By 1820, just as the Industrial Revolution was gathering pace, the average Indian earned just 43 per cent of the average European and the average Chinese managed 49 per cent. Indian per capita incomes declined during the eighteenth century, not just in relative terms but even in absolute terms, due to the turmoil that accompanied the dissolution of the Mughal empire. The Industrial Revolution caused the gap to widen at an accelerated pace. By 1950, India had a per capita income that was just 14 per cent of Western European levels. Devastated by war, the average for China was even lower at 10 per cent. Again, the data is consistent with a view that India began to fall behind from the eleventh century and that colonization and the Industrial Revolution merely speeded up the process.

Over the last millennium, India went from being an economic and cultural superpower to becoming virtually irrelevant. This is why 1991 is potentially such an important turning point—it could mark the reversal of a trend that has lasted a thousand years.

Why Did the Indian Civilization Go into Decline?

India had maintained its position as a cradle of civilization and a lynchpin in the global trading system for a remarkably long time. Indeed, it did this for longer than any country before or since. Why then did it go into such a sharp decline after the eleventh century? It is tempting to simply blame it on repeated foreign invasion—by Turks, Mongols and Afghans from Central Asia and later by European colonial powers. Between AD 1000 and 1025, Mahmud of Ghazni made seventeen raids into northern India. Then, following Muhammad Ghori's victory in the Second Battle of Tarain in 1192, waves of invaders from Central Asia subjugated the subcontinent. The Muslim conquest of India was undoubtedly a very bloody affair—temples, universities and cities were laid waste and hundreds of thousands, perhaps millions, of people were massacred (anyone who doubts this should read *Tarikh-i-Farishtah*[12]). The impact on India's social fabric was harsh and it led Nobel laureate V.S. Naipaul to call India a 'wounded civilization'.

However, this alone does not quite explain the secular decline of India as a civilization and a leading world power. India was no stranger to foreign invasion. Over the centuries Huns, Bactrians, Indo-Greeks, Sakas and others had invaded India. Their invasions must have caused disruptions but did not cause a long-term decline in the country's fortunes. The Indians had put up a spirited resistance to these incursions— the Gupta and Mauryan empires had both risen in response to external threats. Even when the invaders had penetrated deep into the country, India had simply absorbed and assimilated these groups into its larger fabric; Indian civilization lived on. In the case of the post-eleventh century invasions too, India successfully absorbed many elements of Islamic culture. However, the country's relative position went into secular decline. What had changed?

In popular perception, the Muslim conquest of India was the result of a young and vigorous religion defeating an old pacifist civilization. This is why it is seen as having been especially disruptive. However, this is hardly borne out by the sequence of events. Hindu India was quite able to fend off Muslim incursions for hundreds of years. During the period of the great Arab expansions of the seventh and eighth centuries, the Muslims conquered an empire that ran from the Iberian peninsula to the borders of India. They defeated with ease many of the great powers of the time including the Sassanians of Persia and the Byzantines. Yet, despite repeated attempts, they were unable to expand into India beyond a tiny toehold established in Sind in the early eighth century. It would be another four centuries before Muslims would be able to hold territory in the Indian heartland. Meanwhile, several Hindu warrior kings like Bappa Rawal led successful military raids against the Muslims during this period and the Hindu Shahi kings continued to rule over most of Afghanistan well into the tenth century. In fact, Indian military technology was considered very good and was used by the Muslims against the Christian Crusades (particularly, the metallurgical techniques used to produce the so-called 'Damascus sword').

In short, Hindu India proved quite capable of holding its own against the vigorous new religion at the height of its power. Even after the Muslim conquests of the thirteenth century, the continued resistance of the Rajputs of Mewar, the kingdom of Vijaynagar and the Ahoms of Assam in later centuries could not be faulted for lack of spirit or courage. The 'religious vigour' theory, furthermore, does not explain the subsequent failure of the descendants of these same Muslim invaders (now Indian but still Muslim) to fend off later invasions from Central Asia as well as their poor resistance to European colonization. Again, one cannot fault the likes of Tipu Sultan for lack of courage.

The main factor that seems to have let down Indians, whether Hindu or Muslim, appears to have been growing technological naiveté after the eleventh century—which shows up, for instance, in the willingness to deploy lumbering war-elephants against arrayed artillery as recently as the eighteenth century. However, this gap shows through in all facets of human endeavour, from economic and mercantile prowess to scientific and philosophical enquiry. Even the great Mughal edifices were built without the use of a wheelbarrow but through the mass deployment of brawn. In the end, it is more reasonable to argue that it was civilizational decline that led to foreign domination rather than the other way around. The individual brilliance of a few great monarchs, such as Akbar and Krishnadeva Raya, was not able to reverse the secular long-term decline. As eminent historian Tapan Roychaudhuri puts it: 'In terms of ideas and attitudes, mid-eighteenth century India was not at all that different from the country described by Marco Polo.'[13]

It is difficult to establish precisely what caused this fossilization. However, a key factor appears to have been the erosion of the spirit of entrepreneurship and the openness to new ideas and enquiry. There are several independent signs of intellectual fossilization around the eleventh century. The most direct comes from the writings of Al Beruni, an eleventh-century scholar who lived in the court of Mahmud Ghazni and wrote a remarkable book on the India of his time. While Al Beruni is not entirely a neutral commentator, some of his comments provide an interesting insight into contemporary Indian attitudes to knowledge and science. Take for instance: 'Their haughtiness is such that, if you tell them of any science or scholar in Khurasan and Persis, they will think you to be both an ignoramus and a liar. If they had travelled and mixed with other nations, they would soon change their mind, for their ancestors were not as narrow-minded as the present generation.'[14] Al Beruni goes on to quote a passage from Varahamihira in which the ancient Indian thinker gives credit to the scientific contributions of the ancient Greeks.

Al Beruni lived in the court of Mahmud of Ghazni and was probably commissioned by him to write the book on India. Clearly Mahmud took the trouble to learn about his victims. This is what allowed him to make seventeen raids into northern India between AD 1000 and 1025 without eliciting a successful response from a country that was still a major economic power. Perhaps it is significant that the Indians did not bother to write an equivalent book about Ghazni.

The process of decline appears to have first taken root in the north and then spread southward. For instance, we know that in the early eleventh century the Chola empire in the south was at its height both militarily and culturally. However, writings by later travellers suggest that the closed attitude towards technology, new ideas and the outside world had spread throughout the subcontinent by the thirteenth century. Writings by Ibn Batuta and Marco Polo show how India had fallen behind the rest of the world. Contrast this with the writings of earlier Chinese and Greek travellers. Not surprisingly, this backwardness began to have a palpable impact on the country's maritime trade and economic prowess. Take for example Marco Polo's comments regarding international trade in the Malabar coast in early fourteenth century:

'Let me tell you next that this country does not breed horses. Hence all the annual revenue, or greater part of it, is spent in the purchase of horses. You may take it for a fact that the merchants of Hormuz and Kais, of Dhofar and Shihr and Aden, all of which provinces produce large numbers of battle chargers and other horses, buy up the best horses and load them on ships and export to this king and his four brother kings. Some of them are sold for 500 sagi of gold, which are worth more than 100 marks of silver. And I assure you that this king buys 2000 of them or more every year, and his brothers as many. And by the end of the year not 100 of them survive. They all die through ill usage, because they have no veterinarians and do not know how to treat them. You may take it from me that the merchants who export them do not send out any veterinarians or allow any to go, because they are only too glad for many of them to die in the king's charge.'[15]

As this passage shows, the greater part of the country's export earnings were being wasted as a consequence of the lack of a very basic technology (and a technology that had been known in earlier times but appears to have been lost). This same closed attitude also shows through in social mores. For instance, caste rules from this time begin to ostracize those who sailed overseas. It is not surprising that from here on, Indian merchants ceded ground to the Arabs, the Chinese and eventually the Europeans in the Indian Ocean.

The injunction against crossing the seas embodies an astonishing reversal of attitudes for a civilization that had once been at the centre of the world's most important maritime trade system. These rules survived well into the early twentieth century. When my great-grandfather decided to do his doctorate at the London School of Economics in the early 1920s, the family priests forbade him from travelling abroad. Fortunately, he was not one to give in so easily. According to family legend, he spent several weeks studying the holy books and proceeded to prove to the priests that the scriptures did not contain any injunctions against crossing the seas.

But why did the Islamic invasions not trigger a change in attitude? The Muslims did bring in new technologies (most visibly in architecture, food and warfare) but change seems to have been in the nature of a level shift rather than in the process of inquiry. It is very difficult to gauge why this was so, but the most plausible explanation is that by the time Muslim rule was firmly established in India in the thirteenth and fourteenth centuries, Islamic civilization itself was past its peak. By this time, Christian armies had begun the re-conquest of the Iberian peninsula while the Mongols had laid waste the Middle East. As Professor Pervez Amirali Hoodbhoy puts it: 'One gets the impression that [Muslim] history's clock broke down somewhere during the fourteenth century and that plans for repair are, at best, vague.'[16]

By the end of the fifteenth century, Columbus would have discovered the Americas and Vasco da Gama would have turned the Cape of Good Hope and landed on the Malabar coast. Within a few short decades the tiny European nation of Portugal would have established a stranglehold on the Indian Ocean from Aden to Malacca. Portuguese power would eventually give way but, over the next four centuries, a succession of European powers would dominate Asia—the Dutch, the French and most importantly the British. The Muslim world would never again challenge the West militarily or intellectually.

The Importance of a Culture of Openness

The important point is that the cause of backwardness was not so much a problem of intellectual capability but of cultural openness to ideas and risk-taking. The same people, who were capable of inventing algebra and calculus in the fourth century, were unwilling to learn the relatively simple technology of maintaining horses in the thirteenth century. Once it had been a culture that celebrated its merchant fleets but later forbade crossing the seas.

Of course, India is not the only civilization to have gone into decline because of its cultural inability to generate and internalize new ideas and technologies. China too suffered the same fate. It is well established that in the early 1400s, China's naval technology was generations ahead of Europe. Admiral Zheng He led a series of expeditions that visited South-East Asia, India and East Africa. There is some speculation that his fleet may even have visited the Americas. Certainly, his ships were capable of making the journey.

It took the Europeans another three hundred years to re-invent much of the ship-building technology that was used by

Zheng He. Yet, it was not the mighty Chinese but 'barbarians' from Europe that would dominate global trade over the next five hundred years. Again, it was not due to the lack of initial scientific capability but due to negative cultural attitudes. China's mandarins did not deem the rest of the world worthy of their interest. Zheng He's *Treasure Fleet* was burned down and its records deliberately suppressed. Eventually, the knowledge accumulated by the voyages was forgotten and the country's technological capabilities stagnated and then went into decline. By the eighteenth century, the country was clearly far behind Europe. Thus, it was a change in cultural attitudes towards innovation and the outside world that led to technological stagnation and eventually to economic and civilizational decline.

Western civilization too had gone through a similar cycle following the decline of the Roman Empire in the fifth century. In that case too, civilizational decline had been the result of changed attitudes. As the early Christian church consolidated its power over the Roman Empire in the fifth century, it systematically shut down the centres of learning and persecuted scholars for being too 'pagan'. The library of Alexandria—the greatest store of knowledge in the ancient world—was deliberately destroyed by Christian zealots in the late fourth century. In AD 415, the Greek philosopher Hypatia, one of greatest woman mathematicians of all time, was killed by a Christian mob in Alexandria. A few schools struggled on for another century till Plato's academy was shut down under the order of Emperor Justinian in AD 526. The few scholars that escaped the persecution would take their knowledge and their books to the Middle East, where under the protection of the early Muslim caliphates, the knowledge of the ancients would be rediscovered. It would be another thousand years until scholars like Galileo would challenge the Church in Europe and usher in the Renaissance.[17]

It appears that civilizations, from time to time, commit suicide by closing themselves to innovation, entrepreneurship and the outside world. It is not clear why advanced civilizations sometimes chose deliberately to go backwards. ·However, the fate of the Sanskrit language provides a good guide to how Indian civilization became fossilized.

The Story of Sanskrit

Language is a reflection of a civilization. It is the medium through which people formulate and express their ideas. Therefore, the evolution of a language mirrors the development of the corresponding society. If there is any language that embodied ancient India, it is Sanskrit.

Today we tend to think of Sanskrit as a static language that is used mainly for formal religious ceremonies, rather like Latin is used in Roman Catholic countries of Europe. However, in ancient times it was an active and vibrant language that was used for activities ranging from poetry and drama to science, philosophy, law and mathematics. It was so successful because over the centuries it underwent enormous change in order to accommodate evolving intellectual and social requirements.

First, it must be recognized that Sanskrit was part of a continuum of mutually intelligible dialects. Sanskrit was merely the formal end of the spectrum and was used for legal, academic and administrative purposes. It was also the medium of formal religion and high literature. At the other end of the spectrum were various Prakrits that were spoken in everyday life. Their very names tell the story—Sanskrit literally means cultured or perfected while Prakrit means natural. The point is that Sanskrit was not an isolated and ring-fenced tongue but was a part of a larger milieu.

Second, Sanskrit was constantly evolving and adding

vocabulary. The ancient Sanskrit of the *Rig Veda* (compiled in the third millennium BC) is in many ways closer to ancient Iranian rather than to the language of the epics *Ramayana* and *Mahabharata* (probably composed between 1000 and 800 BC). In turn, the language and vocabulary of the great epics is very different from that used by Kalidasa during the Gupta empire of the third to fifth century AD. Throughout these centuries Sanskrit happily absorbed new words and usages from other languages including ancient Dravidian, Munda and probably even Greek.[18] Many words that are thought to be Sanskrit words appearing in modern Dravidian languages like Tamil are probably ancient Tamil words that made their way to Sanskrit.[19] In fact, the language was evolving in so many directions that from time to time it had to be standardized by grammarians like Panini in the fifth century BC and Patanjali in the second century BC.

The periodic standardization was very important in the development in Sanskrit. Panini's efforts created a formal language that was used by the educated from Central Asia to the South China Sea. Panini himself was not strictly Indian but what we would today call an Afghan. Unfortunately, over the centuries, the guardians of the language became increasingly preoccupied with the purity of form and vocabulary. More and more grammars were written and the rules became an end in themselves. The language stopped absorbing new words. Eventually Sanskrit was killed by over-regulation. Contrast this with the fate of the unregulated Prakrit dialects that continue to thrive today as modern Indian languages like Hindi, Gujarati, Marathi, Assamese, and Bengali. Clearly internal over-regulation proved to be far more deadly than foreign domination.

The fate of Sanskrit mirrors that of medieval India. All societies need rules to function effectively. Traditions and rituals provide meaning and a common social idiom. Unfortunately, the intellectual and political leaders of medieval India became increasingly obsessed with regulating everything. There were rules for castes, rules about food, rules for professions, rules for religious rituals, rules for crossing the seas, rules about auspicious time. Rules, rules, rules. Some of these rules had ancient origins but they increasingly became obsessive.

In the end, India closed off its mind and regulated itself into centuries of decline. Of course, there were moments when Indian civilization would briefly show sparks of its former brilliance but even the exceptions prove the point. The Taj Mahal was built by a half-Mongol emperor and his Persian architects. This does not make the structure any less beautiful or any less Indian. Unfortunately, the Muslim invasions did not tear down the web of regulation but added an additional layer of rules; and this milieu was still in place when the British embarked on their conquest of India. It was only in the early nineteenth century that this web of social and intellectual regulation began to slowly break down.

The Nineteenth-century Reawakening

The Portuguese were the first Europeans to establish trading posts in India. They were followed by many other Europeans— the Dutch, the French, the Danish and the British. However, till the mid-eighteenth century, these were no more that tiny enclaves. This changed after the British East India Company acquired Bengal after the Battle of Plassey in 1757. Over the next several decades the East India Company came to directly or indirectly control most of the subcontinent. The British may have conquered India for their own commercial/imperialist purposes but they did have a very positive long-term impact on

India's 'wounded civilization' by introducing India to modern institutions, science and the English language. Most importantly, they created a environment where a number of remarkable individuals were able to set about unshackling the Indian mind.

Perhaps the most important of these early reformers were Raja Ram Mohun Roy and Ishwar Chandra Vidyasagar, both Bengalis who lived in the first half of the nineteenth century. By this time, the glories of ancient India were mostly forgotten. The great works of Aryabhatta, Charaka and the Vedic philosophers had not been entirely lost but they were learned by rote, without thought to their meaning. Even the short-lived liberal vibrancy of Mughal Emperor Akbar's sixteenth-century court was a fading memory. The disintegration of the Mughal empire had left the country in chaos during the eighteenth century. Ram Mohan and Vidyasagar now set about reconstructing the civilization from its ashes.

Ram Mohun Roy was fluent in several languages including Bengali, Hindi, Arabic, Persian and Sanskrit but he realized that a true renaissance would only be possible by the country being provided with a means to access the new ideas emanating from the West. Therefore, he fought for the introduction of English in Indian schools and for the teaching of 'modern' subjects like Human Anatomy and Mathematics.

The importance of the English language in rekindling India cannot be understated. The language played a very important role in not just opening the country to new ideas but in the rediscovery of its own past. For the first time since the decline of Sanskrit, educated Indians had a common language capable of conveying new ideas. Its introduction by the British may have been a matter of convenience for the colonial power but, as will be discussed more fully later, the leading Indian reformers of that time were strongly in favour of English.

Vidyasagar was one of the first products of the new approach to learning. He came to Calcutta (now Kolkata) from a remote village to study at the newly opened Sanskrit College in 1829. Over the next few years, he taught himself the ancient Sanskrit texts as well as English and Hindi. Having imbibed the spirit of renaissance, he went on to make major contributions in areas ranging from women's rights and education to Indian language publishing. He even simplified the Bengali script and gave the language its modern form. He is said to have been responsible for the establishment of numerous schools for girls and helped found Calcutta University, the subcontinent's first modern university, in 1857.

Ram Mohan Roy and Ishwar Chandra Vidyasagar were followed by a series of brilliant reformers including Dadabhai Naoroji, Gazulu Chetty, Madhav Ranade and Swami Vivekananda. In virtually every case they were products of the new education system and lived in the 'British' cities of Madras, Calcutta and Bombay. The old 'Indian' cities of Delhi, Hyderabad and Lucknow produced few reformers.

Most importantly, these nineteenth-century reformers were all very conscious of the need of a wider civilizational re-awakening. Over the next century, their idea of cultural modernization led the Independence movement. Note that throughout this period, the country's intellectual leadership continued to emphasize the need for innovation and cultural openness. Ram Mohan Roy's intellectual successor, Nobel laureate Rabindranath Tagore wrote this famous poem in his *Gitanjali* collection (published in 1913):

Mind Without Fear (translated from Bengali)

Where the mind is without fear and the head is held high;
Where knowledge is free;

Where the world has not been broken up into fragments by
    narrow domestic walls;
Where words come out from the depth of truth;
Where tireless striving stretches its arms towards perfection;
Where the clear stream of reason has not lost its way into
    the dreary desert sand of dead habit;
Where the mind is led forward by thee into ever-widening
    thought and action—
    Into that heaven of freedom, my Father,
        let my country awake.

Unfortunately, Tagore's warning against 'narrow domestic
walls' was not heeded by post-Independence India. Instead the
leadership opted for an inward-looking approach that retarded
the re-emergence of India for another half-century. The inward-
looking strategy is sometimes justified today as having been
the fashion of the time but a leader of the stature of Nehru
should have been able to look beyond contemporary fashion.
By opting for a closed economic system, he unwittingly
perpetuated a very ancient mistake that went back a thousand
years and had played an important role in causing India's
decline.

However, it is not fair to just blame the Gandhi–Nehru
dynasty and the Congress party because most of their political
opponents were no better. There were many who accused
Nehru and the Congress of not going far enough. Moreover,
the failure was not merely limited to economic thinking but
extended to all spheres of life. In an extraordinary act of
cultural policing, it was decreed that all representations of
Tagore's works had to be done according to prescribed
formulae. This is particularly striking since Tagore had dedicated
his life to encouraging innovation in literature, art and
education. Thus, it was a failure of virtually the entire political
and intellectual leadership of post-Independence India. Perhaps,
it was the weight of 'dead habit' reasserting itself.

2

From Independence to Freedom

When India became independent in 1947, there were many competing visions of how India should develop. These ranged from Mahatma Gandhi's vision of self-sufficient villages to those of the Soviet-inspired Communists. Although the Congress was by far the largest party or political organization, it contained several strong personalities and their sharply differing views. However, as Prime Minister Jawarharlal Nehru came to dominate the Congress into the fifties, it was he who forged the path that India eventually took.

Perhaps the most visible manifestation of the Nehruvian Vision during the post-Independence period was an inward-looking economic arrangement that used a complex system of bureaucratic controls in order to allocate domestic resources and to minimize contact with the rest of the world. It was first mooted in 1948 and then formally proclaimed in the Industrial Policy Resolution of 1956. The private sector was tolerated but strictly held in check by industrial licenses, while the public sector became the centrepiece of national policy. A Soviet-inspired Planning Commission was established and series of Five-Year Plans were set in motion.

Mahalanobis and His Mechanical Toy

The system was originally the brainchild of one of Nehru's closest advisors—the statistician Prashanta Chandra Mahalanobis—who devised a 'scientific' input–output model that aimed to speed up the country's development through State intervention. It was a static mathematical model in which the economy took in raw materials and spat out finished goods. All that needed to be done was to collect statistics for the demand for goods and then coordinate the supply of inputs through a system of government control and licensing.

The whole approach was based on a mechanical view of the world that simply assumed away the role of private enterprise. There was no place in this model for the messy, organic process of risk-taking and innovation that drives economic progress. Technology was seen as an external input that could be mandated by the mandarins of the Planning Commission rather than as a process of generation and diffusion of new ideas. Unfortunately, Mahalanobis did not appreciate the fact that all economies are evolving eco-systems that have less in common with Newtonian mechanics and more with ecological biology—mutations, symbiotic interlinkages, changing equilibria and the survival of the fittest. These dynamics cannot be meaningfully reduced to statistical input–output models.

Most damaging of all, the model tried to minimize contact with the rest of the world. The external world was merely a residual that was grudgingly and temporarily tolerated to take care of all that could not be provided within the country. Over time, a process of import-substitution was expected to reduce the country's dependence on the rest of the world. It reflected a mentality that feared the world and wished to protect itself by shutting it out.

Speaking in the presence of Prime Minister Nehru at the Indian Statistical Institute, Calcutta, on 3 November 1954, Mahalanobis said:

> 'Work is already in progress on a 12 sector model (that is, a 12 X 12 table) . . .'

Thus, India's future was decided on the basis of a statistical table with twelve columns and twelve rows. In today's age of computers, this is something that even a ten-year-old can do on an Excel sheet. Unfortunately, it seems to have impressed a lot of people in the fifties. The only constraint that was correctly judged by Mahalanobis was the lack of trained personnel. However, even here, he was unable to get away from his static world-view of input–output models:

> 'In dealing with the programme of industrial production one of the most important questions would be an adequate supply of trained personnel at all levels. This may indeed prove to a serious bottleneck . . . Input–output tables in respect of manpower will be of help in this connection.'[1]

In other words, the whole education issue was merely a matter of adding in an extra row in the model. The input–output approach did lead to investment in education but of a very peculiar kind. Rather than invest in the general primary education, the country used up all its education budget to provide specialized personnel for grandiose public-sector projects (we will return to this subject in a subsequent chapter).

Despite all these obvious shortcomings, the Mahalanobis model had the big advantage that it gelled with Nehru's own Fabian Socialism. This does not mean that Nehru was ignorant of the need to infuse the Indian economy with new ideas and technology. He was a learned man who was more than aware of India's historical experience. However, his approach was to inject new technology into India by using large public-sector projects such as the Bhakra Nangal dam cum irrigation system. He termed such projects as the 'temples of Modern India'. When inaugurating the Nangal canal in July 1954, he said: 'Then again it struck me that Bhakra Nangal was like a big university where we can work and while working learn, so that we may do bigger things.'[2]

Unfortunately, these mega-projects were no more likely to trigger a sustained renaissance than Emperor Shah Jahan's building of the Taj Mahal in the seventeenth century.[3] At best they could be a one-time infusion of particular techniques but they were never likely to generate a self-sustaining dynamic of enquiry and risk-taking. Nehru and Mahalanobis did not understand innovation. In particular, they did not understand that innovation is necessarily an unpredictable process that comes about through the millions of little and great interactions between people. These cannot be dictated by input–output models and industrial licenses. Therefore, what matters is to create an open culture with institutions that encourage interaction within society and with the outside world. Their economic approach was the modern-day equivalent of the ancient caste-rules against crossing the seas. By introducing bureaucratic control over this process and limiting contact with the rest of the world, Mahalanobis created the very 'narrow domestic walls' that Rabindranath Tagore had warned against. This is especially ironic since he had personally known Tagore and had briefly worked as the poet's secretary.

Mahalanobis's 'scientific' model had the same impact on the economy as the learned punditry of the medieval grammarians had on Sanskrit. As a consequence of the import-substitution policies, the next two generations of Indians were condemned to sloppy and outdated goods and services—although they could have a false pride that these shoddy products were all 'Made in India'. As a child growing up in the seventies and eighties, I do not remember ever having purchased anything that was not domestically produced.

Meanwhile, public-sector monopolies ran everything from airlines to telecommunications, banking and food distribution. These monopolies were originally set up on the pretext that the Indian private sector was not mature enough to supply these goods and services. In many cases, however, the authorities created the public-sector monopolies by simply expropriating the private sector. This process of nationalization accelerated after Nehru's daughter Indira Gandhi came to power in 1966.[4] She was driven down this path partly by ideological preference and partly by political instinct. The banking system, for example, saw three waves of nationalization. In 1955, the State Bank of India and its associates were nationalized. Then, another fourteen commercial banks were nationalized in 1969 and a further six were taken over in 1980. Thus, by the early eighties, the government controlled virtually the entire banking sector.

This was not all, almost all other major financial institutions were also owned by the State. The existing life insurance companies were all nationalized in 1956 and amalgamated into the Life Insurance Corporation of India. The largest mutual fund (Unit Trust of India) was government owned as were the major term-lending institutions like the Industrial Development Bank of India. Thus, the government effectively extended its control over all resource allocation within the country. In each case of nationalization, it was argued that financial institutions controlled by the private sector would not meet the development goals of the country. In practice, the political leadership then proceeded to pilfer the resources of the nationalized banks by blindly handing out loans to the 'people' and to fund pet projects. Credit was given out to politically important groups at 'loan melas' with little thought to creditworthiness. Indeed, many of those who received the monies would have been entirely surprised to learn that there was any expectation of repayment.

The private sector was not entirely dismantled. Instead, it was tied up in a Kafkaesque system of licensing, regulation and taxation that precluded all enterprise. The income tax rate at one point in the seventies stood at 97.25 per cent! A plethora of government licenses were required if a private-sector company wanted to expand capacities even in existing product lines. Heaven forbid that they should want to introduce a new product. What mattered was not innovation and efficiency but the ability to lobby with the government for the much sought-after licenses. In turn, this reinforced the political power of those who controlled the process and encouraged them to introduce ever more regulation.

The result was a world of chronic shortages and shoddy goods and services. A Public Distribution System was built up—a network of ration-shops meant to distribute basic necessities like sugar, rice and kerosene at a reasonable price. Most of these rationed items were perpetually in short supply due to the inefficiencies of the government-controlled procurement and distribution systems. When these goods were available, there were serious problems with quality because most of the good stuff had been pilfered along the supply chain and sold in the black market. In fact, a small industry developed in order to produce specialized substances that could be used for purposes of adulteration (for instance, white sand and gravel for the adulteration of rice).

A telephone connection was considered a luxury that required years of waiting. The trials and tribulations of the lucky telephone owner were not over once he/she had acquired the coveted instrument. Lines were frequently down and required to be fixed—which required regular 'encouragement' for the State telephone-department employees.

The restrictions on the establishment and operation of a private-sector enterprise were equally tedious. Before making an investment, the entrepreneur was first required to get an approval in principle from the Ministry of Industry. If the ministry agreed, usually after many visits to its offices, it issued a Letter of Intent. This merely allowed the entrepreneur to apply to various departments for a plethora of other approvals. If he wanted to import machinery, for instance, he had to apply to the Chief Controller of Imports and Exports in the Ministry of Commerce. The approval for this was, however, given by a committee that was actually under the Ministry of Industry. If there was need for a foreign technology collaboration agreement, the businessman had to get an additional approval from a committee chaired by the Finance Secretary but serviced by the Ministry of Industry. A large number of files drifted back and forth within the government, and often simply got lost.

Meanwhile, if the entrepreneur also wanted to raise capital from the markets, he had to approach the Controller of Capital Issues. If he wanted raw material, he had to apply on an annual basis to the Commerce Ministry. Each time, the Director General of Technical Development had to certify that the imports were not available indigenously. After all this had been tied up, the entrepreneur went back to the Ministry of Industry for the 'Industrial License'. Unfortunately, this was not deemed good enough. After the enactment of the Monopolies and Restrictive Trade Practices Act of 1969 (MRTP), the harassed entrepreneur had to apply separately to the Department of Company Affairs for a separate MRTP clearance.

The above examples of bureaucratic red tape are merely an illustration of how the licensing system worked.[5] In practice, there were a myriad other rules and regulations. Large numbers of industries were reserved for the public sector. There were also many industries that were reserved for the small-scale sector. The system led to delays, corruption and inefficiency. With little incentive and scope for innovation and expansion, the Indian private sector became fossilized. The symbol of Indian entrepreneurship of this period is the Ambassador car produced by Hindustan Motors. Based on the Morris Oxford, the car used reasonably up-to-date technology when it first came into production in 1958. However, a largely unchanged version of the Ambassador remained the mainstay of the Indian automobile industry till the late 1980s. The only choice was a car based on a 1962 Fiat design produced by Premier Automobiles. In other words, by the mid-eighties, the only available automobiles had barely changed in a generation.

This does not mean that Indians were totally unaware that they were being short changed. Foreign goods were actively smuggled in and were available in the black economy, often openly displayed in markets with colourful names like 'Fancy Bazaar' and 'Heera-Panna'. These were clearly of better quality than the Indian-made goods and were sold at exorbitant prices to the relatively wealthy. The combination of extortionate tax rates and smuggling created a parallel economy that is estimated by some to have amounted to 50 per cent of the official economy and over 70 per cent of the non-agricultural sector in the eighties.[6] Well-known economist Raj Krishna cynically described the resultant mix of public sector and the black markets as 'socialist allocation in the first round followed by market allocation in the second round'.

Not surprisingly, growth and development floundered. Economic growth averaged around 3.5 per cent per annum from 1950 till the late seventies. This rate of GDP growth was famously dubbed by Professor Raj Krishna as the 'Hindu rate of growth' although it would have been more accurate to call it the 'Nehru–Mahalonobis rate of growth'. The pace of economic expansion was barely higher than the pace of population growth during this period (around 2.1 per cent per annum) and, not surprisingly, failed to raise standards of living for the vast majority of the country's populace. Furthermore, the system was very unstable and prone to frequent macroeconomic breakdown—as demonstrated during the crises of 1966-67, 1974-75, 1979-80 and finally in 1991.[7] Meanwhile, the import-substitution policy made India irrelevant to the rest of the world economy. The country's share in global trade declined from 2.2 per cent at the time of Independence in 1947 to barely 0.4 per cent at the eve of liberalization in 1991.

It should be noted that this failure was not merely a matter of excessive government intervention but that of closed-minded isolationism. Many governments in East Asia and Latin America intervened in their economies during the fifties, sixties and seventies. However, there was a big difference between those that remained open and those that decided to close themselves. The Latin Americans typically opted for an import-substitution model where they, like India, closed themselves off from the rest of the world. The result was decades of slow growth, debt and default. In contrast, East Asian countries typically leveraged State support to build up infant industries to take on world markets. In South Korea and even relatively developed Japan, initial government support was important in building up successful private-sector exporters. Singapore went a step further and built up world-class companies from within the public sector (for instance, Singapore Airlines). The difference was that at a time when the Indians were forcing out multinational companies and weighing down its talented professionals and entrepreneurs, Prime Minister Lee Kuan Yew was welcoming them with open arms. Openness, as always, was the critical difference. As India would itself discover later, even the public sector performs better in an open and competitive environment.

The Failure of Vision

Apologists for Mahalanobis and Nehru argue today that they were merely following the advice of the leading Western economists of that time, such as Joan Robinson and Ambassador John Kenneth Galbraith. This is partly true but the blind following of fashion is no excuse for poor judgment. Moreover, it is also usually forgotten that many well-known international and Indian economists had also warned against the use of one-dimensional models for economic planning. Take for instance the interesting comments of Milton Freidman, who later became a Nobel laureate, on Mahalanobis, in 1956:

'Mahalanobis began as a mathematician and is a very able one. Able mathematicians are usually recognized for their ability at a relatively early age. Realizing their own ability as they do and working in a field of absolutes, tends, in my opinion, to make them dangerous when they apply themselves to economic planning. They produce specific and detailed plans in which they have confidence, without perhaps realizing that economic planning is not the absolute science that mathematics is.'[8]

Great men often make great mistakes, and they should be held accountable for them.[9] This is especially true for Nehru who deliberately sidelined those who argued against the inward-looking import-substitution model. Take, for example, Chakravarthi Rajagopalachari, a stalwart of the Congress party and the last Governor-General of independent India till it became a republic in 1950. Together with Sardar Patel and Nehru, he had been amongst Mahatma Gandhi's closest advisors. He had even been the leading contender to become the country's first President.

When Nehru began to shift towards increasingly socialist policies, Rajagopalachari strongly opposed him. However, he and his supporters were sidelined as Nehru consolidated his power-base (Sardar Patel, the other stalwart, was also opposed to Nehru's socialism but died in December 1950). With little room to manoeuver within the party, Rajagopalachari left the Congress in 1957. Two years later, at the age of eighty, he and Minoo Masani formed the Swatantra Party to advocate liberal economic policies. Unfortunately, after some initial success in the sixties, the party faded away as geo-political circumstances pushed the country's intellectual and political focus ever more to the Left.

The above discussion largely deals with the economic system of the pre-liberalization world. However, it was a cultural attitude that pervaded every sphere of life—from domestic politics and academia to foreign policy. The political arrangement that developed from this milieu combined populism with patronage, and the political leadership openly used state-control over economic resources to maintain and exercise power.[10] Prime Minister Nehru himself may not deliberately have set out building this structure but he certainly presided over its creation. This system of political patronage specifically targeted the financial sector, but it was true of all sectors of the economy. Thus, there was a direct and reinforcing relationship between the economic and political arrangement.

While researching this book, I found that many commentators take the stand that the country's political economy was quite clean under Nehru and only deteriorated under his daughter Indira Gandhi. There is nothing to suggest that either Nehru or Mrs Gandhi were deliberately building up the system of corrupt patronage. To blame the problem entirely on the personal integrity of Nehru's daughter, however, is to trivialize the problem. It was a major failure of vision and of the fundamental logic of centralized bureaucratic control and import-substitution. The problem certainly snowballed into a monster under Mrs Gandhi's watch but she merely took the system to its logical culmination. Indeed, many of the problems blamed on the Indira Gandhi era were visible from the very beginning.

Take for instance the infamous Mundhra Scandal in 1957, just a year into the Second Five-Year Plan. The State-owned Life Insurance Corporation was accused of having made irregular investments in a Kanpur-based firm owned by businessman Haridas Mundhra.[11] The issue was raised in Parliament by none other than Feroze Gandhi, the Prime Minister's estranged son-in-law and Indira Gandhi's husband. When the Finance Minister's evasive replies did not satisfy anyone, the scandal forced the government to institute a number of independent enquiries headed by eminent judges. The report from the judges was damning and Finance Minister Krishnamachari was forced to resign. My grandfather, a senior advocate at Allahabad High Court, was one of the lawyers then given the responsibility to unwind the web of financial transactions. The incident clearly illustrates that the dangers of government involvement were visible from the very onset.

By the mid-sixties, there was growing evidence the import-substitution model was not working. As Gurcharan Das[12] points out, 'For every control that failed, we needed two more to shore up the original one.' Despite these obvious shortcomings, very few people other than the Swatantra Party questioned the whole arrangement. While some businessmen like J.R.D. Tata may have grumbled, it is remarkable how few intellectuals opposed the system. The few who did, such as Professor B.R. Shenoy, were loudly denounced and sidelined.

The Price of Geo-politics

Many developing countries, including many in Asia, dabbled with state-led development strategies in the fifties and sixties. However, India was not just obsessively inward-looking but also responded to growing signs of failure in the sixties by intensifying government control. Why, as the economy floundered in the sixties, did the country not change course?

Unfortunately, a sequence of political events within and without pushed India further to the Left. Internal squabbles within the Congress party led to a split in 1969. Indira Gandhi was forced to seek the support of the Left parties in order to remain in power. Mrs Gandhi naturally leaned towards State-control but now it was a matter of political survival. She embarked on a series of populist moves, including nationalizing banks, to shore up her support base. Then, matters came to a head on India's eastern border.

Since Independence, West Pakistan had politically and economically dominated the eastern wing of the country (what is now Bangladesh). As a result, dissatisfaction had been building up against the military dictatorship. The relationship sharply worsened when severe floods in 1970 caused great devastation but elicited an apathetic response from the national leadership based in newly built Islamabad. When elections were finally held in December 1970, East Pakistan voted en bloc for the Bengali nationalist Awami League. Since East Pakistan had more than half the overall population, the Awami League got an overall majority. The prospect of being ruled by a Prime Minister from the East was not acceptable to the West Pakistan elite who 'cancelled' the elections. East Pakistan broke into open revolt.

The military government of Yahya Khan responded by sending in the troops. The result was a genocide in which an estimated three million people, especially intellectuals and minorities, were killed. The residential halls of Dhaka University were particularly targeted. Up to 700 students were killed in a single attack on Jagannath Hall. This was a genocide on a scale comparable to Pol Pot's Khmer Rouge but is today barely remembered by the rest of the world. Between 1970 and 1971, between eight and ten million refugees poured into eastern India. My father was one of the officials in charge of providing relief to the refugees. On the day I was born, my father was out with Prime Minister Indira Gandhi visiting refugee camps in the borderlands of Twenty-Four Parganas District which had been affected by serious floods. Amidst the mounting chaos, and given the poor communications of that time, my mother had no idea where my father was. The next morning, the front page of the leading newspaper had a photograph of my father and the Prime Minister supervising relief efforts.

The evolving crisis elicited an unforgivable response from Western governments. Rather than pressure the military dictatorship in West Pakistan to stop the genocide, President Nixon repeatedly threatened Indira Gandhi and eventually sent in the US Seventh Fleet to cow her. Strengthened by the political support from the US, Pakistan's military commanders ordered a pre-emptive air strike on India, code named Operation Chengiz Khan, on 3 December 1971. The Indian response was swift and sharp. Within twelve days, Indian troops and Bengali rebels had forced the Pakistani forces in East Pakistan to surrender. Thus, Bangladesh was born.

The birth of Bangladesh was the most obvious result of the events of 1971 but the sequence of events had an equally large impact on the Indian psyche. Western support for Pakistan in the face of blatant political suppression and genocide disillusioned India and pushed it towards the USSR. The US Seventh Fleet had brought back memories of the fleets of the East India Company. It was a purely symbolic gesture since the United States was already bogged down in Vietnam but Nixon's response created a suspicion of the West that would remain engrained for a generation. India had long flirted with the Soviet Bloc but now Mrs Gandhi clearly tilted towards it.

In embracing the USSR at its hour of need, India ended up mixing its geo-politics with its economics. Rajagopalachari died in 1972 at the age ninety-four and with him died the Swatantra Party and its advocacy of liberalism. It faded almost completely from public memory and few people today remember the party or its leaders. I tracked down the last vestige of the Swatantra Party to a tiny office in Mumbai's Kala Ghoda. It has only one remaining member, S.V. Raju who has kept the party alive all these years in the hope that one day its time will come.

Geo-political convenience, unfortunately, did not resolve the fundamental economic problems of the country. The economy continued to flounder and there was growing political unrest. Prime Minister Indira Gandhi infamously declared an Emergency in 1975. She assumed dictatorial powers and suspended the democratic process. Many leading opposition leaders were thrown into jail. Mass protests, however, continued. Eventually, fresh elections were held in 1977. The long-incumbent Congress was defeated and replaced by the Janata Party, a rainbow coalition of various opposition groups.

The Janata Party, unfortunately, did not represent a different economic vision. Their ire was directed personally at Mrs Gandhi rather than at the underlying framework. Indeed, there were a number of die-hard socialists within the alliance and the Industrial Policy Statement of 1977 sought to further widen the scope of the public sector and increase the restrictions on private enterprise. Thus, the regime's economic policy is now best remembered for the expulsion of Coca-Cola from the country. This is why India's economic failures cannot be blamed entirely on the Nehru–Gandhi dynasty. Almost the entire political/intellectual elite was in favour of State control. Some groups, such as the Communists, wanted even more government intervention.

The Eighties and the Promise of Reform

The Janata government collapsed after two years due to internal squabbles and the Congress party under Mrs Indira Gandhi came back to power even as the economy was hit by major shocks—a jump in international energy prices due to the Second Oil Shock combined with a severe drought. GDP fell by 6 per cent in financial year 1979-80, which meant that per capita income fell by over 8 per cent—a very big shock for a poor country like India.

Faced with these shocks, the new government attempted to ease supply-side restrictions. Yet another Industrial Policy Statement was issued in 1980. This time, the government decided to regularize capacity expansions that had taken place without the necessary licenses. This was small victory for the private sector but some commentators see it as the turning point. From now, there were some tentative attempts to improve the efficiencies of the public sector and even to introduce new technologies. For instance, the period saw the advent of colour television and national transmission (introduced just before the Asian Games held in Delhi in 1982). This would go on to have an important impact on the Indian public consciousness.

Then, in October 1984, Mrs Gandhi was assassinated by her bodyguards. I was in middle-school in Kolkata at that time and remember how the teachers stood speaking in hushed tones in the corridors. We were all sent home. There were soldiers on the streets and rumours of riots. The situation in Delhi, of course, was much more tense. The event unexpectedly put a young Rajiv Gandhi at the helm. He won an overwhelming majority in the national elections held a few months later.

For the first time there was some talk of economic reform. In December of that year, the public-sector Maruti Udyog introduced new automobile models under collaboration with Japan's Suzuki.[13] Over the next few years, these new models— particularly the Maruti 800—took over Indian roads. This was a major socio-economic revolution. Virtually all Indians of my generation will remember where they first encountered the bright-red Maruti 800 and, for the lucky few, when their parents first purchased one.

The Maruti 800 was a frugal affair with an engine that produced barely 37bhp and an ambitious top speed of 120km/h. However, it was a major milestone for a people who had been deprived of international technology and quality for over a generation. Predictably, there were a few sceptics in the beginning who argued that the new-fangled technology would never survive the flooded streets and potholes of an Indian monsoon. They were proved wrong and the country fell in love. It was common to see large families of six or seven stuffed into the tiny vehicle with perhaps a couple more hanging out of the hatchback.

Meanwhile, GDP growth too accelerated in the eighties to

5.4 per cent[14] from the Nehru–Mahalanobis level of 3.5 per cent witnessed during the previous three decades. The combination of higher growth and tentative reforms has led some observers to argue that India's liberalization process began much before 1991[15]. While this is technically true, it should be remembered that the essential features of the socialist system were left untouched. In fact, it can be reasonably argued that some distortions worsened during the second half of the eighties. Even the acceleration in growth during this period is suspect because it was not due to widespread improvements in efficiency but due to the willingness to run up ever larger domestic and external debts. Between 1980 and 1991, India not only saw its external debt jump from US$16 billion to US$85 billion, but also witnessed a significant deterioration of the maturity profile of the debt. The government ran large deficits and the combined debt of the state and Central governments rose from 51 per cent in 1981 to 69 per cent a decade later. In the end, the eighties growth-pattern proved unsustainable and ended in a serious external crisis.[16] Even the introduction of Maruti 800 would have been no more than a one-time injection of technology but for subsequent events.

It is not the tentative reforms and growth acceleration of the eighties that are remarkable but the astonishing loyalty exhibited by the ruling elites and the intelligentsia to the import-substitution model in the face of its glaring shortcomings and, by now, the obvious success of the outward-oriented emerging economies in the rest of Asia. Of course, there were a few dissenters but they were a small minority. The main debate was largely about how to iron out the niggling problems of the existing arrangement rather than about the irrationality of the system as a whole. So when Prime Minister Rajiv Gandhi famously commented that only 15 per cent of monies spent on anti-poverty programmes actually reached the poor, it was a comment about corruption and inefficiency and not really a repudiation of the system itself. The overwhelming opinion was that the Nehruvian Vision had not been correctly implemented and not that it was fundamentally flawed.

I do not want to leave the readers with the impression that the period from 1947 to 1991 was one of total darkness. There were areas of progress. Till the sixties, India had been prone to severe food shortages whenever variations in weather caused crops to fail. Disaster was averted mostly due to large-scale international aid (under the PL-480). This began to change in the seventies as the 'green revolution' introduced new seed varieties and significantly increased production of certain foodgrains. Basic literacy rates rose from 18 per cent in 1951 to 52 per cent in 1991. Even if it was slow, per capita incomes also did rise at 1.5 per cent per annum between 1950 and 1980, and then at double that pace in the eighties. Infant mortality declined and average life expectancy drifted up.

However, these achievements pale in comparison to what had been achieved by the rest of Asia. Literacy rates in China in 1991 stood at 81 per cent, Indonesia's stood at 82 per cent, South Korea's stood at 96 per cent and Thailand managed to increase it to 93 per cent. The difference in per capita incomes was even more dramatic. The average Indian in the early nineties lived on less than a dollar a day. The average Thai had an income level that was five times higher and that of the average South Korean was twenty-three times higher! Yet, all these countries had been roughly at India's level of development when it became independent. In fact, China had been significantly poorer.

The Collapse

Despite these obvious shortcomings, the socialist economic system lasted till 1991—briefly surviving the fall of the Berlin

Wall in 1989 and then collapsing along with the Soviet Union. It is worth noting that when change eventually came, it was not due to an ideological change amongst the political and intellectual elites. The country's leadership did not voluntarily change course and, intriguingly, was under no domestic political pressure to do so. In the face of overwhelming evidence of failure, the country's intelligentsia stayed loyal to the 'Vision'. Years after the Berlin Wall had fallen and even after India itself had initiated economic liberalization, economics undergraduates at Delhi University were still being taught about the wondrous benefits of the Mahalanobis model and about Preobrazhenski's arcane ideas regarding producer surplus. As students, we could not help being struck by the disconnect between what we were expected to learn in class and what was happening in the real world around us.

What eventually caused the system to collapse was not, therefore, a change of heart but a major economic crisis. The proximate factor that tipped India into the balance-of-payments crisis was an increase in global oil prices due to the Iraqi invasion of Kuwait in August 1990. With the First Gulf War looming, the price of crude oil jumped from US$15 per barrel in July to US$35 per barrel in October. The cost of oil imports escalated even as dollar remittances from Indian workers in the Gulf took a hit. At the same time, the domestic political situation was deteriorating. The V.P. Singh government collapsed in November when the Bharatiya Janata Party withdrew its support in Parliament. A minority government led by Chandra Shekhar assumed power for a few months with the help of the Congress, but it too collapsed by March 1991. National elections were announced for May.

Faced with such uncertainty on both economic and political fronts, expatriate Indians began to withdraw their money from special non-resident deposit schemes. Foreign exchange reserves continued to decline despite support from IMF funds and the ratings agency Moody's downgraded the country. It was clear by the beginning of 1991 that the country was sliding into an external payments crisis. A new agreement with the IMF in January for an additional US$1.8 billion did little to stabilize confidence. A number of measures were put in place to squeeze imports but reserves continued to haemorrhage. The country was teetering on the edge of default. In desperation, the government pawned twenty tons of gold to Union Bank of Switzerland in order borrow US$200 million. Gold is seen as a symbol of honour and trust in India, and pawning it was tantamount to national humiliation.

Then, in the midst of the election campaign, Rajiv Gandhi—former Prime Minister and leader of the Congress party—was assassinated by a suicide bomber. The election schedule was postponed to June. When the results were finally announced, the Congress party emerged as the largest party but still short of a majority in the Lok Sabha (Lower House of Parliament). Without Rajiv Gandhi to lead it, the party recalled veteran politician Narasimha Rao from virtual retirement to lead a minority government. He faced a daunting economic situation: inflation was running at 13 per cent and rising, the current account deficit was running at US$10billion, and foreign exchange reserves were barely worth two weeks of imports. The country's external debt now amounted to 250 per cent of exports, compared to 150 per cent a decade earlier.

Prime Minister Rao fatefully decided to appoint Dr Manmohan Singh, a former Reserve Bank governor, as his Finance Minister. With Rao's backing, Dr Singh dismantled some of the worst features of the *ancien régime* over the next two years. Industrial licensing was virtually abolished, tax rates were rationalized, the private sector was freed from the tyranny of the MRTP Act and the complex import control regime was torn down. Public-sector monopolies were ended for sectors ranging from airlines to banking. Restrictions on foreign portfolio and direct investment were eased. The exchange rate was depreciated in stages to more competitive levels and then was put on a 'managed float'.

The immediate results were astonishing—foreign exchange reserves rose sharply, growth accelerated, and the economy stabilized. However, the reforms of 1991–93 were not just about macroeconomic stabilization. It was about taking the first step towards freeing India from its old isolationism. For the first time in a millennium, India had the courage to face the real world—to compete in global export markets, to attract foreign investment, and to allow the messy hustle-bustle of free markets. Even more importantly, it opened itself intellectually and culturally to the outside world—a precondition for economic prosperity as well as a socio-cultural renaissance. As we shall see in the next chapter, the year 1991 saw the unwinding of a mindset that was irrationally suspicious of the outside world and of innovation, that abhorred entrepreneurship and risk-taking and, above all, that was paralyzed by an ancient fear of failure.

Therefore, it is more than likely that future generations will see 1991 as a turning point that was at least as important as 1947 and perhaps more. China provides a good analogy since Deng Xiaoping's reforms in the seventies and eighties can now be said to have proved to be more important to China's destiny than Mao's revolution of 1949. Yet few Indians today would equate the importance of 'independence' from foreign rule with 'freedom' from the inward-looking mindset. Even Narasimha Rao and Manmohan Singh, the two main architects of the reforms, were at pains to justify the changes of 1991 within the old Nehruvian framework.

In his Budget Speech on 29 February 1992, Finance Minister

Manmohan Singh felt it necessary to say: 'Our nation will remain eternally grateful to Jawaharlal Nehru for his vision . . .' However, he knew that he was treading into dangerous territory for he concluded his speech by saying, 'Tonight I feel like I am going to the theatre. Let the assassins be informed, I am prepared for their onslaught.'[17]

The 'assassins' responded soon enough. A few days later, Communist leader Somnath Chatterjee spoke passionately against the new regime in his speech at the joint session of Parliament: 'The Narasimha Rao government, now headed by a sober-gentleman-turned-arrogant, will go down in history as the one which has mortgaged our country to the imperialist financial marauders for some tainted lucre.'[18]

Even the Congress party itself did not present the reforms as an achievement as it would have meant having to vilify its previous policies. Thus, even those who were responsible for the reforms, remained unwilling to emphasize the importance of 1991.[19] Indeed, once the immediate Crisis period was over, they sharply slowed down the pace of reforms despite the clearly visible benefits of the new regime.

Why are present-day Indians shy of fully recognizing the importance of 1991? A possible reason for this is that the changes were forced on the country at a moment of failure. Unlike in 1947, there had been no heroic struggle against foreign rulers. Unlike Mahatma Gandhi and other stalwarts of the Independence movement, Rao and Singh are not looked on by most Indians as great heroes. Both of them had been leading members of the old regime and had been forced by circumstances to initiate the liberalization process. The fact is that India has attained 'freedom' despite the wishes of its political elite and its intelligentsia. More intriguingly, the middle class—which had the most to gain from change—was initially ambivalent and did not provide the strong political support needed by the reformers. Why? We will return to this later.

Nonetheless, we should give credit where credit is due. Prime Minister Rao and his technocrat Finance Minister must be commended for having had the courage to disband the very system that had built them. Some credit should also be given to IMF and other donors who pressured the government to initiate liberalization. The IMF is usually vilified for its role during emerging market crises. Often these criticisms are valid. However, the institution can be justly proud of how it handled the Indian external crisis of 1991. Lastly and most importantly, credit must be given to India's entrepreneurs who, despite some initial trepidation, grabbed the new opportunities. We now turn to their story.

3

The Entrepreneurial Explosion

There is one crucial difference between the two historical moments of 1947 and 1991. The year 1947 represents a clean break from the past. In contrast, 1991 is more like a turning point, the beginning of a process that goes on to this day. The Narasimha Rao regime did implement a flurry of important changes in the first two years of liberalization. However, as the economy bounced back from the Crisis, it lost the sense of urgency. Since then the reform process has been gradually moving forward—a great deal of promise, some implementation and even the occasional retreat. On one hand, there are instances when the pace quickened—Finance Minister Chidambaram's bold 'dream budget' in 1997 and then during the later years of Prime Minister Vajpayee's BJP-led government. On the other hand, there have been instances where the process has ground to a halt.

Nonetheless, the cumulative gain of this gradual

liberalization has been very significant when viewed from the perspective of a decade and a half. The tax regime, for instance, is now much less onerous even if it is still far from ideal. Restrictions on foreign investment have been whittled down. Even the Chief Minister of the Communist-ruled state of West Bengal now woos investment from foreign multinationals. While full-fledged privatization has been patchy, the public sector is now under much greater competitive pressure due to private-sector entrants into once-protected markets.

However, the most important change has been the explosion of entrepreneurial activity. It is important to have some sense of this process in order to fully comprehend the new order that has emerged. For purposes of discussion, it is useful to divide up the first fifteen years of liberalization into three five-year periods: 1992 to 1997, 1998 to 2002 and finally 2003 to 2008. While there are common threads that pass through all three, each time-period has distinct characteristics that had a bearing on the particular economic trajectory taken by the Indian economy.

The First Phase: The First Breath of Freedom

The first phase (1992–97) began with the initial burst of reforms. The process was initiated by the 'Statement of Industrial Policy', presented on the 24 May 1991, which did away with most industrial licensing and the burdensome restrictions of the Monopolies and Restrictive Trade Practices Act on firms. It also ended the public-sector monopoly over many sectors and allowed for automatic approval for foreign direct investment up to a 51 per cent stake. The industrial policy statement was followed by a number of other measures. Foreign institutional investors were now allowed to invest in the Indian equity markets. Even more importantly, the external trade regime was rationalized. Quantitative controls were removed even as import tariffs were lowered. The peak import tariff rate before liberalization had stood at a prohibitive 355 per cent. This was lowered to 85 per cent by 1993 and then to 50 per cent by 1995. As the protection of tariff walls fell, domestic industry was compensated by devaluing the rupee to more competitive levels.

The Indian private sector seized the opportunities long denied to it. After a lull of half a century, a new breed of entrepreneurs emerged to take advantage of the opportunities. This was an important development because the socialist era had fossilized the private sector and had not allowed new blood. With the notable exception of Dhirubhai Ambani of Reliance, most of the big businesses were still controlled by families that had their roots in colonial times—the Tatas, the Birlas, the Bajajs and so on. Therefore, the 'creative destruction' of a market-based economic system was simply unknown to the Indian business world. That changed between 1992 and 1997. Brand-new companies appeared in sectors as diverse as airlines, mass media and banking.

The airline industry had been nationalized under the Air Corporations Act of 1953. As a result, the country had only two public-sector airlines: Air-India for international flights and Indian Airlines for domestic travel. The two initially had reasonably good service standards but by the eighties they were just as bloated and inefficient as the rest of the public sector. Then, in 1994, the Air Corporations Act was repealed. In the next few years a slew of new domestic airlines appeared— Jet Airways, Damania, East-West, ModiLuft, Air Sahara. Indian travellers were all of a sudden treated to flights that were affordable and to smartly dressed cabin crews who served with a smile. Not all the new airlines would survive the competitive environment but that is to be expected in a liberalized world. A few survived and thrived. Most notably Jet Airways would go on to create one of the best managed and fastest-growing domestic airlines in the world. A decade later it would be leading a pack of private Indian airlines competing for international routes.

Government control over the financial system was an important ingredient of the socialist system of resource allocation and political control. Loans were often based on politics rather than economics. As a result, the banking system was stuck in a quagmire of non-performing loans and inefficient operations. This was recognized by the reformers as a major problem because the banking system (and the financial system generally) plays a role similar in the economy to that which the circulatory system plays in the functioning of the human body.

The government set up a committee under former Reserve Bank Governor Narasimham to look into the matter. The committee submitted its report in November 1991 and, on its recommendation, a number of changes were initiated—the system of arbitrary administered interest rates was unwound in favour of a market-oriented system, the pre-emptions through directed lending were rationalized, prudential norms were tightened and new private-sector banks were allowed to be established. Between 1993 and 1998, ten domestic private-sector banks and fifteen foreign banks entered the market. These had computerized records and nice air-conditioned offices—a huge improvement on the old dusty offices of the public-sector banks with their long queues and piles of old files.

While many of the new growth sectors were a result of explicit changes in regulations, others took off merely because the new spirit of openness gave entrepreneurs confidence that their businesses would not be damaged by future attempts by the government to control them. The cable TV industry is an excellent example of how a major sector spontaneously emerged during this period through the efforts of thousands of small entrepreneurs in an unregulated market.

Television was first introduced in India in 1959 on an experimental basis by the State-owned radio on the back of a UNESCO grant. These efforts eventually led to the establishment of the State-owned Doordarshan in the seventies. Transmission was in black and white and programmes were often oriented to 'social education' rather than entertainment. A frequent prime time programme was *Krishi Darshan* (literally translated to Views of Agriculture) that usually featured an 'expert' who waxed eloquent on the relative merits of various fertilizers. The authorities appeared not to have noticed that the transmission was limited to a few major cities and that virtually no farmer could afford a television set. To be fair, there were also programmes that aimed to entertain. Perhaps the most popular show was *Chitrahaar* which showed music clips from Hindi films. Adults and children alike waited all week to see their favourite stars sing and dance. Occasionally, a popular film would be shown. Those who owned television sets will remember how the entire neighborhood would turn up to watch the movie.

The eighties saw a steady change. Nationwide colour transmission was introduced at the time of the Delhi Asian Games in 1982. Aided by the successful launch of geostationary INSAT satellites, Doordarshan began to beam commercially sponsored soaps such as *Hum Log* which turned out to be a huge success. By the end of the decade, a nascent production industry had developed to supply Doordarshan with popular programmes. Serialized renditions of the epics *Ramayana* and *Mahabharata* proved to be immensely popular. Nonetheless, the State-owned channel was still the only available route and choice was severely limited.

All this changed in the early nineties with the advent of cable TV. It all started when a few enterprising operators in the late eighties set up video players and wired up their apartment blocks to show popular films. It was an isolated affair limited to a few middle-class neighbourhoods in the largest cities. Then, during the first Gulf War, a few hotels in Mumbai and Delhi decided to put up satellite dishes to telecast CNN. Soon thereafter, Hong Kong-based Asia Satellite Telecommunications launched AsiaSat and a number of foreign-owned channels like BBC, MTV and Rupert Murdoch's Star began to beam channels into India. A few Indian language pioneers like Zee TV soon joined them. The local cable operators caught on to this and, within a flash, they were criss-crossing their neighbourhoods with rooftop cables. For less than US$2 per month, Indians could have unfettered access to a growing number of channels and pirated film videos.

The cable operators were neither regulated nor organized. These were small businesses run by the local electrician, or even the neighbourhood goon. There were turf wars between rival operators, familiar neighbourhood boys-turned-entrepreneurs pleaded with residents to subscribe to their services rather than those from the next street. They undercut fees, and promised to beam pirated versions of the very latest Hindi films. There were even reports of how turf battles led to bloodshed although competition was more peaceful in most localities. By the mid-nineties, cable TV was ubiquitous in urban India and was fairly common even in rural areas. Thus, in the blink of an eye, the most basic form of private enterprise had created one of the largest cable TV markets in the world.

The government was not unaware of these developments. In early 1991, an internal report of the Ministry of Information and Broadcasting is said to have commented that 'Programmes specifically targeted at Indian audiences are likely to be beamed from foreign satellites in the near future'.[1] In an earlier era, the government would have reacted to this by trying to ban the phenomenon on grounds of 'national security'. However, attitudes changed with liberalization and it decided to opt for benign neglect. Legislation would later attempt to consolidate and structure the sector, but there would be no serious attempt to control the medium.

Given this boom in entrepreneurial activity, the economy recovered quickly from the Balance of Payments crisis. GDP growth bottomed out in financial year 1991-92 at 1.8 per cent and then bounced to over 5 per cent in the next two years and then accelerated further to register over 7 per cent between 1994 and 1997. These were unprecedented growth rates for India—more then twice the Nehru–Mahalonobis level. At the same time, other macroeconomic indicators too improved dramatically. Foreign exchange reserves, which had dipped to less than US$3 billion in April 1991, rose sharply to over US$25 billion by April 1995. Similarly, the external debt ratio stabilized and then began to decline. Foreign portfolio inflows began to flow into the country and the stock markets and real-estate prices rose sharply. Overall, this was a dramatic turnaround for a country that had almost been in default at the beginning of the decade.

Nonetheless, not everything went well. The economy had been liberalized under duress and the underlying institutional structure was not prepared for the new environment. For instance, the sharp increase in the stock market attracted not just investors but also fraudsters who tried to profit from institutional inadequacies. In 1992, the stock market was hit by a major financial scandal involving banks and a number of well-known brokers including 'Big Bull' Harshad Mehta. It transpired that they had siphoned off funds from the banking system to speculate on the stock market. When this scandal became public, the stock market declined sharply and Harshad Mehta was arrested.

A year later, the state government of Maharashtra signed a deal with Enron to build a power plant in Dhabol. It was, at that time, the largest foreign investment deal that had been ever signed in India. However, the deal was not transparent and signed in a hurry. The project soon got bogged down in accusations and counter-accusations of corruption and mismanagement. More than a decade later, the Dhabol deal was still being debated in the courts (in fact, long after Enron itself had ceased to exist). Both these episodes show that Indian officials still needed to learn how to deal with the new world.

By the end of the first phase, the systemic inefficiencies of the Indian economy were beginning to show. The physical infrastructure was poor and incapable of dealing with high growth. Existing public- and private-sector companies were finding it difficult to deal with an environment where new players and imports could contest former monopolies. Meanwhile, the reform process itself had ground to a halt. Once the immediate crisis period was over, Prime Minister Rao and Finance Minister Manmohan Singh decided to ease off— presumably under pressure from the old guard within their own party. In 1996, the Congress lost the elections and was replaced by a motley coalition headed by Prime Minister Deve Gowda. Thereafter, the progress on reforms became even more erratic although there were a few bright spots (such as Finance Minister Chidambaram's attempt to simplify the tax structure).

The Second Phase: The Pain of Restructuring

Despite the slow pace of reforms, the second phase (1998– 2002) was an important period as it saw the impact of liberalization percolate through the economy. During the previous phase, many of the systemic inefficiencies were papered over by the economic boom. By the late nineties, competition from new entrants and imports was palpable. This was not just true of the public sector. The old business families had long complained about the licensing regime but many of them were not prepared for the new environment. Most of the incumbent private-sector companies were run by family members or old family retainers rather than by professionals. For more than a generation there had been no incentive to innovate and take risks or to attract and reward talent. Faced with competition, some of the leading industrialists publicly complained about liberalization and even argued for special protection for specific sectors.

Fortunately, there was enough support for reforms that they continued forward at a slow pace. Market pressures began to force the public and private sectors to restructure themselves, adopt new technology and revamp management. The Tata group of companies was one of the first to embrace change. It was one of the few that already had a professional cadre of managers—the Tata Administrative Service. The cadre had been established by the legendry J.R.D. Tata in the 1950s. He had been Nehru's personal friend but had also been one of the few who had dared to publicly criticize his economic policies. Led by JRD's successor Ratan Tata, the conglomerate went through a major restructuring. Between 1996 and 2001, the Tata Iron and Steel Company laid off 30,000 workers or 40 per cent of its workforce while Tata Engineering and Locomotive Company, the automobile manufacturing business, laid off 10,000, or 29 per cent of its workforce.

Soon many of the other old family-owned businesses like the Aditya Birla Group, Mahindra & Mahindra and Bajaj had begun to implement drastic restructuring plans. Even public-sector companies like the State Bank of India began to change due to competitive pressures. Voluntary retirement schemes were used to pare down staffing, workers were retrained, new technologies were introduced and product lines were rationalized. Of course, there was some initial political opposition to these changes. However, the labour force proved to be far more willing to accept the changes than the political elite and intelligentsia had imagined. Ten of thousands of workers were retrenched from the old industrial companies without major labour unrest or indeed major changes in labour laws. In fact, the data shows a sharp decline in mandays lost from industrial action during these years. It was possible because liberalization had brought attitudes that were very different from those of the past. The man on the street recognized the need for change and was willing to take the pain.

What made the industrial restructuring even more painful, however, was the lack of bank credit. The banking system had been used in the pre-liberalization era to fund a number of politically convenient projects. Creditor rights had been very weak and the banks were in no position to seize and liquidate the assets of defaulters, even when some of them blatantly misused credit. The Reserve Bank and other regulators, therefore, began to tighten prudential norms. The banks reacted by cutting bank lending in order to clean up their balance-sheets and stuffed their asset books with government bonds. This preference for safe government securities over lending, termed 'lazy banking' by Dr Rakesh Mohan, caused a credit crunch that seriously hurt the small- and medium-sized industrial units.

Meanwhile, the country was hit by a number of external and internal developments. In 1997-98, the Asian Crisis pulled down many booming economies of East Asia. India was not directly affected by this as it was still a relatively closed economy with significant controls on capital flows. Nonetheless, it affected investor sentiment across the region. At the same time, domestic political conditions became more unstable. Deve Gowda's coalition government fell within a year and was replaced by one headed by Inder Gujral. This government too did not last a year and was replaced by one headed by Atal Behari Vajpayee of the Bharatiya Janata Party (BJP).

Amidst all the political uncertainty, the country also came under increasing terrorist attacks by Islamist groups, including separatists in the state of Jammu and Kashmir. Many of these groups were based in neighbouring Pakistan and in Taliban-ruled Afghanistan. Relations with Pakistan deteriorated with the Indian authorities accusing the Pakistani government of not just tolerating training camps but of actively supporting them. This was before the 11 September 2001 attacks in New York, and international sympathy for India was not forthcoming. Prime Minister Vajpayee decided to signal a more tough stance by testing five nuclear devices in May 1998.

India had long been known to be nuclear-capable. It had exploded a nuclear bomb in 1974. Nonetheless, the world was taken by surprise by the decision to carry out new tests. Pakistan reacted within weeks by conducting its own series of tests. Both countries attracted sharp criticism from the international community and a number of sanctions were imposed on them. Amidst all this drama, the Vajpayee government collapsed in May 1999 due to the withdrawal of support from a key ally. Elections were announced for October.

My elder son Varun was born that summer. Sitting in the maternity ward, my wife Smita and I watched India and Pakistan engage in a 'mini-war' that could easily have spiralled out into a wider conflagration. As the snows melted in the mountains of northern Kashmir (near the town of Kargil), the

Indian Army discovered that some of the strategic mountain-tops along the border had been taken over by Islamist rebels (and, according to the Indian version, regular Pakistani troops). The Indian armed-forces acted to take back the strategic heights. Several hundred men from both sides died in the ensuing conflict before the Indians retook the positions. At its height, there were genuine fears that nuclear-armed India and Pakistan would engage in an all-out war.

The elections in October gave a narrow victory to Prime Minister Vajpayee and the BJP-led alliance (now called the National Democratic Alliance). The NDA government faced an initiation by fire. In December 1999, an Indian Airline flight was hijacked by an Islamist terrorist group to Pakistan and then to Kandahar in Taliban-ruled Afghanistan. The government was eventually forced to release a number of top terrorists in exchange for the hostages. It was a humiliating moment.

Given all these developments, the optimism of the mid-nineties was clearly eroding by the turn of the century. Growth slowed to an average of 5.5 per cent in the second phase, significantly lower than the 7 per cent-plus rates registered in the mid-nineties. With all the restructuring, job growth was slow in the industrial sector. With memories of the 1991 external crisis and the recent Asian Crisis still fresh, the government opted to shore up foreign exchange from expatriate Indians through two schemes—the Resurgent India Bonds and the Millennium India Deposit.

However, the period was not all about political uncertainty and painful industrial restructuring. The services sector continued to grow strongly. Indeed, a number of services sectors that we now associate with early twenty-first-century India first became visible during the second phase—mobile telephony, software, back-office outsourcing, call centres and so on.

The Indian software industry has its roots in the mid-seventies when mainframe manufacturer Burroughs asked their India sales agent Tata Consultancy Services to source programmers for installing system software for US clients. Given the government attitude of the time, it was not easy going. Faqir Chand Kohli, former Vice-Chairman of TCS and considered the father of the Indian software industry, later recalled, 'The government in 1977 in its wisdom applied the Monopolies and Restrictive Trade Practices Act to TCS. It took us three years to get a computer and by that time the computer manufacturer had stopped making it.'[2]

Despite these difficulties, by the early eighties, a number of small software companies were beginning to emerge. In 1981, Infosys was set up as a garage operation by Narayana Murthy and Nandan Nilekani. At about the same time, Azim Premji began to diversify his company Wipro from its cooking-oil and laundry-soap business. However, these businesses would remain relatively small till the mid-nineties. India was just too closed to be able to participate on the world stage. Indian software exports in 1985 were just US$24 million. It is estimated that around 60 per cent of computer science graduates from the prestigious Indian Institutes of Technology left the country during the eighties because the opportunities at home were just too meagre.

Nonetheless, by the early nineties, people within the global IT business were beginning to notice Indian software although it was still small enough to be ignored by the lay person. By 1992, exports had grown to US$164 million, still minuscule compared to what was to come. Infosys in that year had 300 employees and exported US$3.9 million worth of software.[3] The industry continued to grow through the mid-nineties, but two factors completely changed the image of the Indian IT industry towards the end of the decade.

First, the Y2K scare caused a sharp increase in demand for cheap IT professionals. Even if the Y2K problem eventually turned out to be a non-event, it totally transformed the Indian IT companies—it gave them exposure and it allowed them to scale-up rapidly. The rising stock-prices of IT companies during the dot-com boom suddenly created a new class of first-generation millionaires around the world. In India, Narayana Murthy and Azim Premji overnight replaced the old-money industrialists as the faces of the country's corporate sector. The bursting of the dot-com bubble in 2000 did drown some of the weaker players, but the gates into the global business world had been thrown wide open.

Second, and equally important, was the success of expatriate Indians in the Silicon Valley. Names like Sabeer Bhatia (co-founder of Hotmail) and Vinod Khosla (co-founder of Sun Microsystems) became household names in middle-class India during the late nineties. At about the same time, a number of Indian professions emerged to lead major multinationals like McKinsey and Standard Chartered. These success stories gave the Indian entrepreneur a new confidence that he/she could take on the world.

The IT revolution soon began to have spin-offs in the form of IT-Enabled Services (ITES) like call centres, medical transcription, credit-card accounts and so on. According to legend, it all started when American Express decided to set up their credit-card business in the country in 1993. The Amex management in the US were puzzled by the fact that quality was better and costs were significantly lower in the new operation even though it was otherwise very similar to other countries. A year later the bank decided to consolidate their finance functions in three locations around the world. Phoenix, Arizona was chosen as the centre for the American operations and Brighton for the European market. A location was needed for the Asia–Pacific operations. The bank's management remembered the positive reports from India and it decided to establish the Asian centre in New Delhi.

Within a couple of years British Airways and GE Capital Services India had set up large outsourcing units in Gurgaon, a satellite town of Delhi. Thus, the back-office outsourcing industry was born.[4] It is important here to note the importance of being open to the world. Indian white-collar workers had been cheap and skilled even before American Express discovered them. However, they simply did not have a chance in the old autarchic India that frowned on foreign companies and international linkages. Pioneers like Amex and GE still had to battle bureaucracy and poor infrastructure but, by the late nineties, back-office outsourcing units and call centres were being established in ever-growing numbers.

The Third Phase: Take-off

The third phase began around 2003. The national mood at that time was sombre. Years of industrial restructuring and the prolonged shortage of credit had left the country tired. Growth appeared to have slowed, the dot-com bubble had burst and the stock market was down. The BSE Sensex in early 2003 was still running at 3000—roughly at the same level it had been a decade earlier. This was a time that many commentators and academics began to question the gains from liberalization. Some like Arvind Subramanium and Dani Rodrik[5] argued that Indian growth had gone through a one-step acceleration in the early eighties and that the reforms of 1991 had had no discernable impact on economic performance. Others were even more critical. There were scholarly articles in publications like the *Economic and Political Weekly*, a Left-leaning academic journal, that argued that the only real achievement of the liberalization process was to increase industrial unemployment.

Yet, a lot had been achieved by time the third phase began. Both the banking and industrial sectors had been restructured and cleaned. New technologies had been introduced and the labour force had been rationalized. The Vajpayee regime may not have announced too many headline-grabbing changes, but it had steadily introduced a slew of small reforms that were cumulatively allowing dramatic improvements in systemic productivity. By 2001, the coalition government was feeling confident enough to try larger things. An ambitious attempt was made to improve the road network. The Prime Minister announced its plan to create the 'Golden Quadrilateral', a project aimed at creating international quality highways linking the four corners of the country. It was the single largest infrastructure project that the country had attempted since the British built the railway network in the late nineteenth century. At the same time, all major cities began an aggressive programme of building flyovers and intra-city highways.

Unfortunately, most commentators were still very negative on the country's prospects. I remember arguing at investor conferences in 2000–03 that the Indian economy was undergoing productivity changes that would shortly translate into a significant acceleration in growth, and that the country would soon be spoken of in the same breath as China. However, I found it tough going. At seminar after seminar I was told by well-known economists that nothing had really changed. Some went as far as to tell me that my ideas were due to the 'folly of youth' and were coloured by 'rose-tinted glasses'. Fortunately, the message from business was quite different.

After years of restructuring, the corporate sector was finally feeling fit. All of a sudden, there was a feeling that the global success of the software sector could be replicated in other industries. One of the confident new breed was Bharat Forge. Even in the mid-nineties, only a few would have heard of the company or of Baba Kalyani even though both had been in the business for decades. Then, almost overnight, Bharat Forge emerged as a major global supplier of automobile components with clients including Volvo, Daimler Chrysler, Honda, and Toyota. By 2005, it was the world's second-largest forgings company after Germany's Thyssen Krup, with operations across the world.

The new confidence showed through in a number of different ways. For the first time, we now see Indian companies begin to systematically expand abroad and acquire foreign companies. One of the pioneers in this was Tata Tea which bought Tetley, a well-known British tea brand, for GB£271 million (US$475 million) in 2000. This was then considered a huge amount of money and a large step for an Indian company. Within a couple of years, such an acquisition would be considered routine. In early 2007, Tata Steel acquired the Anglo-Dutch steelmaker Corus for US$11.3 billion. For a country that had traditionally feared multinational companies (thanks to the East India Company), the idea of Indian multinationals was an important psychological shift.

Meanwhile, a number of services sectors began to grow explosively. Many of these sectors had come into existence in the previous two phases, but it was in the third phase that they truly begin to scale up. The number of mobile-phone connections was 77,000 in 1995. By 2000, the subscriber base had grown to 3.6 million. However, by early 2008 the number crossed 240 million![6] It was many multiples of the number of fixed-line connections and it has made India the second-largest mobile telephone market in the world.

The software and ITES sectors too came of age in the third phase. The combined revenues of the IT and ITES sector is estimated at US$47.8 billion in 2006-07,[7] a ten-fold increase in less than a decade. Two-thirds of this amount was exports revenues. In 2000, the sector had employed 0.3 million workers. By 2007, it directly employed 1.6 million and is estimated to have created an additional 3 million jobs in various support services. It was no longer a niche activity but a mainstream part of the India that was emerging. Sleepy towns like Bangalore and Gurgaon had become major urban centres and were being discussed in boardrooms around the world.

Another factor that added fuel to the fire was the resumption of bank credit. After having spent the late nineties cleaning out non-performing loans, the banks entered the third phase with balance-sheets that were ready to grow again. Interest rates had declined sharply over the previous decade as inflation had declined and global rates had fallen. The banking sector now began to lend aggressively. The result was the biggest credit boom that India has even seen. After years of credit drought, loans were freely available for purchasing a home or buying a car.

Armed with rising incomes, consumer loans and credit cards, the Indian consumer began to demand a retail experience. In 2000, there were barely any shopping malls in the whole country. Shopping in India had always meant visiting small family-run shops in crowded bazaars. That began to change at the beginning of the decade when Crossroads opened in Mumbai, and Ansal Plaza in Delhi. When they first opened, people flocked to them on weekends to gawk at the lights and open spaces—too dazzled to actually buy things. By 2006 there were several new shopping malls in every major city, and many were under construction even in the mofussil towns.

The combination of all these factors caused growth to sharply accelerate in the third phase. For four years from 2003-04, GDP grew by an average rate of around 9 per cent per annum. India's performance was now second only to China's and the world was paying attention. The stock market reflected the changed perception of the country as foreign portfolio investments began to pour in. In May 2003, the BSE Sensex was running at around 3,000—at roughly the same level it had been a decade earlier. Five years later, it was more than six times higher.[8]

Even those who lived through this period sometimes do not realize the degree of change. The country that had pawned its gold to stay afloat in 1991, now boasted of foreign exchange reserves of almost US$280 billion. This is more than the country's external debt and, therefore, India is now effectively a net creditor to the rest of the world. An economy that had once been dominated by the public sector was now a bustling milieu of private entrepreneurship. In the late eighties, public and private fixed investment had been roughly equal. By 2007, private investment accounted for three-fourths of fixed investment. Before liberalization, imports plus exports of goods and services amounted to less than 20 per cent of GDP but by 2007, their share had jumped to 50 per cent of the economy. In fact, India is now more open than the United States, where exports plus imports amount to just 30 per cent of economy, and comparable to China's 75 per cent.

The Indian Growth Model

India is the latest of a series of Asian countries that have been transformed by economic development in the last half-century. However, India's growth experience in the post-liberalization era was very different from the usual East Asian pattern. The East Asian growth model consists of an export-oriented strategy that uses heavy investment in manufacturing capacity and infrastructure to drive development. The sectors that grow fastest are typically those that use the initially abundant supplies of cheap labour. Thus, these economies usually started out by scaling up low-skill exports like making ready-made garments, toys, cheap household items and so on. With time, they all move up the value chain as wages rise and their workforce become more skilled. Exports shift to things like high-end electronics and automobiles. The services sector becomes an independent driver of growth at a much later stage, if at all.

Japan was the first country to successfully use this strategy to develop but it was followed by the likes of Singapore, Korea, Taiwan and Hong Kong. South-east Asian countries like Thailand, Indonesia and Malaysia also began to apply this strategy from the eighties till the process was abruptly disrupted by the Asian Crisis of 1997. China's recent performance may be dramatic due to its sheer scale and speed but it is merely the latest manifestation of the standard East Asian model.

The Indian growth experience of the last fifteen years did involve rapid internationalization. However, this is where the similarity ends. India did not use its abundant and cheap labour force to scale up low-skill activities. Even before liberalization, India had a skew towards skill-intensive production.[9] However, this skew has become even more pronounced after liberalization. Unlike China which started out by selling cheap toys and t-shirts, India's manufactured exports include complex automobile parts and pharmaceuticals while its rapidly expanding services exports include top-end software and complex back-office outsourcing operations. This is a counter-intuitive trajectory for a country that has a mass of cheap labour and therefore should normally be expected to specialize in activities that use bulk labour. Instead, it appears to have become even more technology and skill-intensive than before. Thus we see growth in sectors like software, airlines, media and finance. Even traditional industries became more skill-intensive after the restructuring of the nineties.

Another key difference with Asian 'tigers' is that India did not see a major acceleration in investment activity till after 2004. As pointed out by numerous studies, heavy investment is a key driver of the usual East Asian model. The most extreme example of the East Asian model is China with an investment rate of around 48 per cent of GDP but virtually all other Asian successes had also experienced a sharp increase in investment and construction activity at the point of 'take-off'. In contrast, the overall fixed investment rate in India was around 22 per cent in 1991 and was roughly at the same level a decade later. This was a very low investment rate by Asian standards and shows through in the poor quality of infrastructure and real estate.

However, the most dramatic difference with East Asia was the sector that generated the growth. In East Asia, export-oriented manufacturing and construction were the boom sectors. In India, in contrast, it has been the services sector that generated the bulk of the growth. The sector has grown so fast that it now dominates the Indian economy, accounting for more than half of GDP.

When the country became independent from British rule, the agricultural sector dominated the economy with a share of almost 60 per cent of Gross Domestic Product. The nascent industrial sector accounted for 13 per cent and the services sector for 27 per cent of the economy.[10] Thanks to heavy public-sector investment, the share of industry grew steadily through the fifties, sixties and seventies. By the beginning of the end of the seventies, the share of agriculture in the economy had fallen to around 41 per cent while those of industry and services had increased to 23 per cent and 36 per cent respectively. This fits the conventional wisdom of the times. Economists such as Kuznets and Chenery had empirically shown that the share of manufacturing rises during the initial stages of development and then falls once the country had achieved a high level of per capita income. This is what also appeared to be happening in pre-liberalization India. The services sector had grown but it was not seen as an independent driver of growth. It grew because of growth in government/ public-sector-related sectors and because of demands for services emanating from other parts of the economy, especially from industry. Indeed, a study by IMF economists suggests that the country's services sector was at that time, if anything, a laggard for its level of income and development.[11]

The tentative reforms of the eighties led to an acceleration of overall growth driven by foreign debt and large fiscal deficits. Although this acceleration would prove unsustainable, it saw the emergence of an independent growth dynamic to the services sector. The sector was still being outpaced by industrial growth but the performance gap was small. This is the time when we see the emergence of first-generation businesses in this sector—small media production companies producing soaps for television, IT companies like Infosys and NIIT, and so on.

Then, the reforms of 1991 ignited the sector. Over the next seventeen years, the sector would grow by an average of 8 per cent per year, far faster than the other two segments of the economy. This was not just restricted to cable television, information technology and telecommunications, however, there were waves of expansion in virtually every services segment— hotels, finance, retailing, airlines, advertising and publishing to name a few. The civil aviation sector provides another good illustration of what happened.

Till the early eighties, flying was the domain of the rich. Long-distance travel essentially meant using the railways. Since the British had built the railway network in the late nineteenth century it had been the backbone of the country's transportation system. For any middle-class Indian who was old enough to remember, holidays meant the clattering sound of the rail-tracks, tea served in earthen cups, the chit-chat with fellow-travellers and the taste of 'railways food' served in stainless steel trays. That world still continued to exist but middle-class India now turned in droves to the air. Soon the old-style trundling railways may no longer hold the special place in the life experiences of future generations (although rail travel will probably come back in a different form).[12]

Of course, one need not get too nostalgic about that world. Railway travel, for instance, came with its own problems—the frequent delays, the poor safety record, dirty toilets to name a few. It is no surprise that the people who could afford to shift to the new airlines did so. In 1991, the number of passengers handled by Indian airports was less than 1.5 million per month. By mid-2007, the country's airports were handling 10 million per month, an almost six-fold increase over the fifteen-year period and far in excess of the designed capacities of the airports. Other sectors like mobile telephony saw even faster growth. Moreover, as each bottleneck was eased, it spawned new business opportunities. The boom in domestic airlines, for instance, led to a parallel boom in hotels, car rentals, travel agents and so on.

The structure of the Indian economy changed drastically as a result of the services boom. By 2007, agriculture accounted for 17 per cent of the economy while the share of industry stood at 26 per cent. The remaining 56 per cent of the economy was generated by services. Thus, the services sector is now larger than the combined strength of the other two sectors. The share of the industrial sector, in contrast, is barely larger than what it was a quarter of a century ago. In other words, the country appears to have shifted from farming to services without having gone through the industrial stage. This not only goes against conventional wisdom but also the experience of other fast-growing Asian economies, particularly that of China where industry and construction now accounts for 58 per cent of GDP and services for 33 per cent.[13]

Why the Indian Model?

There are many possible reasons why India has ended up on this unique growth path and economists are still debating them. Here are the ones that I feel were most significant. First, the economy remained relatively capital-starved through the nineties despite the inflow of foreign money. In East Asia, the investment booms were always backed by very high domestic savings rates. China may have an investment rate of 48 per cent of GDP but it has a domestic savings rate of over 50 per cent of GDP. Thus, it is this large pool of domestic savings that allows the country to fund massive investment projects and still have money left over to fund the US current account deficit. China does not need foreign investment for the capital, it needs it only for technology. In contrast, India's domestic savings rate was flat at an average of 23 per cent of GDP through the nineties.

The resultant scarcity of capital meant that real interest rates were high and the country was forced to use capital sparingly. The banking clean-up of the late nineties made things worse by discouraging the banks from lending freely to the private sector. If finance for industrial investment was expensive, that for consumers and home-buyers was prohibitive. When I purchased my first car in the mid-nineties, I was forced to pay an interest rate of 21 per cent on my car loan! The government could have stepped in to encourage investment but its own finances were in no position to sustain a large spending spree. At one stage the banks' holdings of government bonds rivalled their stock of loans—a classic example of 'crowding out'. Not surprisingly, an East Asian-style investment drive was not tenable in India during this period. Thus, India's entrepreneurs concentrated on those services sectors where they needed relatively little capital and/or could expand without having to depend on government infrastructure spending.

Second, the easing of big-picture impediments like industrial licensing and import tariffs did not get rid of the underlying framework of over-regulation, bureaucratic delays and erratic judicial enforcement. The country had built up a huge baggage of laws, by-laws and regulations at every layer of government during the half-century under socialism. There were even a plethora of outdated laws left over from the British era. This massive body of law did not disappear overnight. What made things worse was that these rules were applied through a civil service and a judiciary that was itself in a state of decay. The judicial system, for instance, takes years and sometime decades to decide on even routine cases.

We will return to these issues in more detail in a later chapter. For our present purposes, it is enough to note that the legal/administrative backdrop remained (and to some extent still remains) stacked against the market economy. However, the lawmakers and civil servants of the pre-liberalization era had largely directed their fury against the agricultural and industrial sectors. The agricultural sector remained burdened by state procurement monopolies and restrictions on internal trade. The industrial sector was overtaxed and over-regulated. The former was the mainstay of the economy and the latter was seen as the upcoming star. In keeping with the conventional wisdom of the time, the services sector was seen as largely incidental. So the services sector was relatively ignored by policy makers and not tied up to the same extent. Therefore, when the macro-reforms began it was in the best position to take advantage of the situation.

Even within the services sector, the ones that did the best were the 'new' activities that were made possible by the dramatic technological changes of the nineties—software, mobile telephone, cable television and so on. Neither the legislature nor the bureaucracy had envisaged these technological shifts and therefore had not bothered to create micro-regulations for them. Thus, a policy change in the top was enough to allow liberalization to percolate down quickly. Take for example labour laws which still discourage employers from hiring workers in manufacturing. Fortunately, these laws do not quite apply to white-collar workers because lawmakers in the pre-reform era had always thought of white-collar as 'management'.[14] Thus, the labour laws were not a major impediment to software companies that wanted to scale up rapidly during the Y2K boom.

The third and possibly most important factor that influenced the unique Indian trajectory was the type of human capital available. Most other Asian countries had tended to expand primary education first, then secondary education and finally tertiary education. Thus, they had high literacy levels at their 'take-off' but a relatively small pool of high-skill workers. It was the opposite in India. Even in the early-nineties, almost half a century after gaining independence, it is estimated that around half the population was illiterate. On the other end of the scale, the needs of the Mahalanobis model has meant that the country had invested heavily in tertiary education and built up a handful of world-class institutions such as Delhi University, the Indian Institutes of Management and the Indian Institutes of Technology.

This dichotomy meant that the bulk of the country's workforce was effectively not employable in anything other than subsistence agriculture. At the same time, there was a middle class that was highly educated but underemployed because of the limited opportunities provided by a closed, socialist economy. Till the late eighties, talented and skilled Indians had two worthy choices—to join the civil services (particularly the elite Indian Administrative Services) or emigrate. Taking the GRE/GMAT and applying to US universities was not so much about gaining new skills but a way to opt out of the system. The resultant brain-drain laid the foundations of successful Indian expatriate communities in the West. Those who remained behind became part of an underemployed pool of cheap white-collar workers. When reforms were finally introduced, the entrepreneurs showed a preference for deploying these easily available skilled workers rather than the relatively unemployable masses.

The globalization of the skilled middle-class was sharply accelerated by the fact that liberalization coincided with the telecommunications revolution. As described by Thomas Freidman in his book *The World is Flat*,[15] technological changes in the last decade of the twentieth century gave a whole new dimension to the process of globalization. It was now possible for knowledge workers sitting in Bangalore and Gurgaon to participate and compete directly in the global economy. In an earlier era, such direct trade in services would not have been possible.

Note that globalization is not a one-way process. Expansions in telecommunications and the electronic media also allowed new ideas and attitudes to spread through the country like never before. It was much more difficult to close off the world when it was being beamed into one's home every day. The resultant changes in expectations and in attitudes towards new ideas are a key part of the larger transformation of India and will be eventually even more important than simply the ability of white-collar workers to compete globally. Naturally the biggest changes in social attitudes and expectations happened in the social group that had the easiest access to the globalizing technologies—the educated middle-class. It was no longer a scandal when talented young men or women decided to give up steady jobs at government departments and set up their own businesses. Parents, who would once have fumed if their daughters stayed out late at friends' dinner parties, are now content to allow their girls to work all night at call-centres or fly to distant lands as air-hostesses.

Thus, globalizing technologies did not merely create the demand for white-collar services but also created the supply. The time had come for the Great Indian Middle Class. In the rest of Asia, sustained growth generated the middle class. In India, it was the middle class that generated growth. It is important, therefore, to look more closely at this group—its genesis and its role in post-liberalization India.

4

The Great Indian Middle Class
and Its Limitations

Origins

The emergence of an active middle class is one of the characteristics of successful economic development. Indeed, the rise of the middle class in Western Europe in the eighteenth century was one of most visible sociological changes triggered by the Industrial Revolution. Just as industrialization transformed the rural peasantry into an industrial workforce, the process also created a demand for clerks, doctors, lawyers, and so on. At the same time colonial empires created opportunities for administrators and military officials. The vigour of eighteenth- and nineteenth-century Britain is often attributed to the emergence of this class as an economic and political force. For the first time, there was a sizeable educated group that applied its intellectual powers to exploration, scientific discovery, commerce, institution-building, literature and so on.

Prior to the emergence of the middle class, these activities had been the preserve of a tiny aristocracy (and sometimes the clergy). The rising middle-class emphasized thrift, education and individual achievement as opposed to inheritance and privilege. Of course, the middle class did not emerge out of a void. A proto-middle class had existed prior to the Industrial Revolution and included petty officials, merchants and skilled artisans. This group had grown during the Renaissance and had become a discernable class by the late seventeenth century, particularly in Britain. However, it was the Industrial Revolution that created the middle class as we know it. Most importantly, industrialization led to urbanization and thereby broke down the traditional hierarchy based on the ownership of agricultural land. Instead, it became possible for skilled and energetic individuals to rise up the social ladder on their own merit. By the early nineteenth century, the middle class was the social group with the most economic power in countries like Britain and France. By the fourth decade of the century, it was forcing political changes in these countries. In Britain, it culminated with the Great Reform Act of 1832 which fundamentally changed the system of parliamentary representation.

The Indian middle-class has its origins in the nineteenth century. A proto-middle class had existed in India for centuries consisting of petty Mughal officials, Bania merchants and Brahmin priests. However, in common with pre-industrial Europe, they did not quite constitute a middle class in the modern sense. It was British rule that created conditions for the emergence of this class. Indeed, its genesis can be traced back to single act—the critical decision to impart higher education to Indians in English.

There is a great deal of controversy around why the British rulers opted for English. The popular view is that the British, self-interestedly, wanted to create a class of Indians who could understand them and help them govern the vast subcontinent. This view is based on Thomas Macaulay's famous 'Minute on Indian Education, 1835' which stated: 'It is impossible for us, given our limited means, to attempt to educate the body of people. We must at present do our best to form a class who may be interpreters between us and the millions whom we govern; a class of persons, Indian in blood and colour, but English in taste, in opinions, in morals, and in intellect. To this class we may leave it to refine the vernacular dialects of the country, to enrich those dialects with terms of science borrowed from Western nomenclature, and to render them by degrees fit vehicles for conveying knowledge to the great mass of the population.'

However, the decision was in reality a complex one and not just a case of a colonial master imposing his language on an unwilling populace. There were many in the colonial administration who disagreed with Macaulay. More interestingly, there were many influential Indians who supported the cause of English. The most prominent of these was a Raja Ram Mohan Roy. He was the first of a series of influential Bengali social reformers who had a major role in modernizing Indian society in the nineteenth century. He was a remarkable man in many ways. By the age of fifteen he was fluent in Bengali, Persian, Sanskrit and Arabic. In 1817 he established one of the first 'modern' educational institutions in the country in Kolkata. It still lives on as the Hindu School for primary/secondary education and as the Presidency College for higher education.

Ram Mohan Roy argued strongly in favour of using English as the medium of instruction in the new educational institutions proposed by the colonial government. Many prominent Indians also supported this cause. This preference for English in a proud and ancient civilization is not as odd as it may seem at first instance. The country has dozens of regional languages, each with its own proud history and literature. However, none of them was spoken across the country nor did they have a ready vocabulary that was capable of conveying the new intellectual advances being made in the West. In ancient times, Sanskrit had been the common language of intellectual interaction in India as well as other parts of Asia (much like Latin and Greek in Europe). It had been used to compose great works in medicine, literature, astronomy and mathematics. However, by the nineteenth century, it had been fossilized for hundreds of years. Over the intervening centuries, Muslim rulers had introduced Persian as the language of administration in many parts of the country but it was no more capable than Sanskrit of conveying the advances of modern science (although its interactions with Hindi led to the development of Urdu which is now the national language of Pakistan).

Reformers like Ram Mohan Roy were acutely aware that India was technologically far behind the West. They correctly blamed technological inferiority as the main reason by their subjugation. Therefore, it was natural for them to demand education in a language that gave Indians access to the best that the West had to offer. The resurrection of Sanskrit would not have served this purpose.[1] India has a long tradition of education and intellectual activity, especially amongst the Brahmins. However, this respect for learning did not mean that Indians necessarily saw education as an active agent of change. As Al Beruni's comments show, by the eleventh century the emphasis had shifted from innovation to scholarly learning. The notion of education as the key to social/economic/political betterment is an important middle-class value that had emerged from the Renaissance in Western Europe and flowered after the Industrial Revolution. The enthusiasm for the English language amongst early Indian reformers like Ram Mohan Roy is a reflection of the new world view.

The middle class grew gradually through the nineteenth century. For the most part it was concentrated in the main cities of Bombay, Calcutta and Madras (now renamed Mumbai, Kolkata and Chennai respectively). Ram Mohan Roy was followed by a string of influential thinkers and reformers such as Vivekananda and Vidyasagar. Although still small in numerical terms the middle class began to have a visible impact on literature, social values, religious practices and national consciousness in general. Leading members of this urban educated middle-class came together in 1885 to form the Indian National Congress. This marks the formal beginning of a movement that would eventually end in independence from British rule. Over the next seven decades, it would be the middle class that would produce the country's leading freedom fighters—Mahatma Gandhi, Subhas Bose, Jawaharlal Nehru and so on. It also produced Jinnah, the founder of Pakistan. Notice how all of them were conversant in English and had studied in England.

Independence and After

Independence opened up a whole new world of opportunities for the educated middle-class. Senior positions in the civil service, the judiciary and the military that had been occupied by the British now became available. At the same time, democracy meant that the old Indian nobility lost control over the patchwork of semi-autonomous principalities that dotted the country. Overnight, the upper-middle middle class became the country's new elite. The Nehru clan is an example of this upward shift.

Then came Nehru's decision to develop the country through

an economic strategy that relied on heavy public-sector investment and administrative guidance. This created even more white-collar jobs in the bureaucracy and in public sector enterprises. However, the government soon hit a major constraint—the middle class was too small to fill all these roles! This should not be surprising since the literacy rate in 1950 was barely 18 per cent. While it is not possible to accurately estimate the size of the educated middle-class at that time, it was probably no more than a couple of million individuals. The scarcity problem was compounded by a skill-mismatch as the government attempted to build large public-sector industrial complexes. These required technical skills while the existing upper middle class was mostly educated in the liberal arts; in line with the British generalist tradition, a typical member of the new elite would have a BA in English Literature from St Stephen's College, Delhi, followed by a degree in Law from Oxford or Cambridge.

As we have seen, Mahalanobis had anticipated this constraint and the government responded by setting up more specialized technical institutes. The elite Indian Institutes of Technology (IITs) were established as part of this effort. IIT Kharagpur was set up in 1951 followed by Bombay (1958), Madras (1959), Kanpur (1959) and Delhi (1961). Many new universities and institutes were established in the early decades after Independence.

Importantly, English was retained as the medium of instruction. There was really no choice because there were no textbooks and technical literature in Indian languages. Besides, the exclusive use of Hindi—which had been envisioned as the national language—was opposed by many. Some opposed it on grounds that it was unfair to the non-Hindi speaking states, and there were vociferous anti-Hindi protests in Tamil Nadu (it would be another generation before most middle-class

Indians would be conversant in basic Hindi). Others took the position that English should be retained as a useful window to the world, especially since it was no longer linked to British colonial rule. As Syama Prasad Mookerjee, a Bengali scholar and the father of the Bharatiya Janata Party,[2] put it: 'If we feel that for all time to come for certain purposes, we will allow English language to be used or taught, we need not be ashamed of ourselves.'

Meanwhile, an elaborate system of written examinations was created to induct students into these new technical institutions and then into the public sector/civil service. An important implication of this process of selection, through mass written tests, was that it sucked in successful candidates from across the country and then reallocated them to educational institutions and jobs in other parts of the country.

This led to the mass housing problem for the newly expanded middle-class. Each employer responded by creating a network of industrial townships and 'colonies' with its own system of graded housing. So, there were colonies for the State Bank of India personnel, for the officers of the Steel Authority of India, for the staff of the Reserve Bank of India, for Army officers, for members of the Indian Administrative Service and professors in the Indian Institutes of Technology. The private sector too replicated this general model and build up industrial townships. In the larger towns, private individuals gathered together to build 'co-operative housing societies'.

It was not entirely a new idea. Such a system of employer-provided housing had existed in British times for some groups like Railway employees. Community-based colonies had also existed such as the Parsi colonies in Mumbai. However, this model was now replicated on a massive scale. Entire towns were built up—for instance, Durgapur in West Bengal was created for the public-sector Steel Authority of India Limited.

Chandigarh was built as the new administrative capital for the state of Punjab (and was later shared with Haryana).

Most employees remained with the same employer all their working lives, and they and their families worked their way up the system of graded housing. Given the predominantly public-sector character of this phenomenon, each age group belonged to the same grade and made its way up the housing ladder at the same pace. This process had a profound impact on the next generation of middle class because it created a pool of middle-class children who had grown up together, played together and had been to the same schools. From the nineties, the demographic profile of the new generation meant that it gradually began to intermarry. The Great Indian Middle Class was coming of age. It is still a work in progress.

Note that this new generation of Indian middle class was very different from the pre-Independence middle class. The identity of the pre-Independence middle class was still rooted in the home provinces. Thus, the Indian middle-class was made up of the Bengali middle-class, the Punjabi middle-class, the Marathi middle-class and so on. This does not mean that they were not proudly Indian (after all, these groups had played such an important role in the national independence struggle) but the regional identities were very strong. The churning described above, however, broke down these identities and created a more pan-Indian identity. I am not suggesting that old affiliations disappeared overnight but merely that we now had a distinct socio-economic group with a shared national outlook and attitude.

The spread of the 'salwaar-kurta' at the expense of the saree is an example of this phenomenon. Just a few decades ago, the salwaar-kurta was commonly worn only in Punjab and other north-western states but today it is the apparel of choice for young middle-class women across India. It is so ubiquitous today that many young women would be entirely surprised to know that an earlier generation would have considered it an unfamiliar apparel.[3]

Meanwhile, the rest of the population had a very different post-Independence experience. The old nobility largely decayed except for those of its members that opted to enter politics or took up some public office. At the same time, the system of industrial licensing and regulation fossilized the business elite. On one hand, it was held back by government control but, on the other, it was preserved from competition. With the visible exception of the Ambani family, virtually no new entrepreneurial family entered the upper classes till the nineties.

At the other end of the spectrum were the hundreds of millions of rural peasants. These groups were largely illiterate at the time of Independence and the founding fathers were keen to given them basic education. The exact system for doing this was largely left to the state governments. Not surprisingly for a newly independent country, most states opted to do this in local languages. Elementary English was also taught but usually at the secondary level (in addition, non-Hindi-speaking states separately also taught the national language). The result was a dual-track education system where the poorer classes were taught mostly in Indian languages and the middle class was mostly educated in English. Language, therefore, became an important barrier. What made this even more inequitable was that the need to fill the technological/ managerial needs of the public sector required ever-growing government subsidies for tertiary education. Thus, the country ended up with a lopsided education system where a disproportionate share of public spending was on English-language-based tertiary education rather than on primary education for the wider population.

Even as the new middle-class took shape in the seventies

and eighties, it was also facing a serious economic challenge. By the late seventies, expansion in public-sector jobs was levelling off. The enthusiasm of the early years had worn off and the inefficiencies of an inward-looking State-led strategy were plainly visible. Opportunities in the private sector were severely limited. The choice was to either compete for the stagnant public sector by taking a series of tough examinations (with a low probability of success) or to emigrate. The talented and the relatively rich opted for the latter option in droves. What had been a trickle in the sixties became a flood by the late eighties. There was a virtual industry around taking examinations like the GRE, SAT, TOEFL and so on. Universities in the US were particularly attractive because of easier financing but many went to the United Kingdom and Canada. A smaller trickle of Indian professionals also went out to the newly rich cities of Singapore and Dubai.

The salaried middle-class was not, of course, the only middle class that existed in the pre-liberalization period. It was an important component of the broader phenomenon and I have used their experience merely as a stylized account. There were many other groups as well—shopkeepers, traders, doctors, lawyers, and even 'fixers' who oiled the government machinery. With the exception of the last category, most professions went through a cycle that mirrored that of the salaried group: a period of expansion and optimism in the fifties and followed by a long period of stagnation.

Small businessmen were particularly demonized by the socialist regime and were seen to be hoarders, profiteers and black-marketeers. A complex system of regulations and 'inspectors' was created to keep in check the suspicious motive of generating profit. Faced with a marginal tax rate that was almost a hundred per cent and a legion of corrupt 'inspectors', small businesses switched their talent from generating profit to hiding it. A large parallel economy emerged. The government responded by adding more regulations but that only increased the parallel economy. By the mid-eighties, both the salaried and the non-salaried middle class were feeling the strain.

The White-collar Boom

When the crisis of 1991 forced change, the middle class was initially ambivalent. It still had a stake in the old system and the opportunities of the new order were uncertain. No matter its initial attitude towards liberalization, India entered the nineties with a middle class already in place that was better educated than was warranted by its stage in development. In other parts of Asia, the middle class had evolved as a result of growth. In mainland China, the nascent middle-class had been largely destroyed by the Great Leap Forward in the late fifties and the Great Proletarian Cultural Revolution in the late sixties. The Chinese middle-class was reborn in the late nineties as a result of sustained growth. The growth process in East Asia was triggered by heavy investment and deployment of cheap labour. The middle class emerged only later as a result and perhaps a force-multiplier.

In contrast, India had a skilled and underemployed pool of white-collar workers waiting for opportunities. Liberalization of the economy led to a burst of entrepreneurial activity, especially in the services sector. First generation entrepreneurs, many from the middle class, emerged from this milieu—Narayana Murthy of Infosys and Prannoy Roy of NDTV are well-known examples of this phenomenon. In turn, they created white-collar jobs for other members of the middle-class. The availability of cheap but educated workers was itself a key factor that encouraged this particular trajectory.

Soon, foreign multinationals also began to set up shop in

cities like Mumbai and Delhi. Together with the new private sector, they began to scout for talent. The numbers were initially quite small, but the entry of foreign consultancies and brokerages broke open the hierarchical 'public-sector' pay packages that had till then characterized even the private sector. The middle-class salaryman was supposed to start as a poorly paid trainee and then slowly work his way up the salary and housing ladder over the next thirty-five years. In keeping with the socialist ethos, it made very little difference if one was talented and hard-working. Once one had made it past the selection process, it was a straight road to retirement. No longer.

In 1993, a well-known foreign consultancy offered a salary of Rs 37,000 per month plus bonus to a fresh MBA from one of the Indian Institutes of Management (around US$13,300 per year at the existing exchange rate). This was front-page news. The salary was more than what a senior civil servant then earned after decades on the job. Old timers shook their heads. The foolish foreign companies had no idea what they were doing. I remember being told by a well-established industrialist that the new kids on the block were spoiling the market by overpaying and were unnecessarily inflaming the expectations of his employees.

Despite widespread resentments, however, there was no looking back. A few years later came the dot-com boom and overnight there were several IT millionaires in their late twenties and early thirties. Most of them came from the middle class. The number of people who initially benefitted from this boom may have been small, but there was a mindset shift as the Indian middle-class realized that it could compete globally. Despite the dot-com bust in 2000, the services boom continued. Domestic sectors like banking, airlines, mobile telephony and hotels scaled up at an unprecedented rate. Externally oriented segments too saw major changes as the narrow software industry broadened out to the wider IT-enabled industry. Call centres mushroomed in the boom towns of Gurgaon and Bangalore. Now there were jobs everywhere.

Manpower Shortages!

In the initial years, the increases in salaries were limited to the highly skilled and the exceptionally talented. There was a lot of slack in the middle-class labour market and it is fair to say that overall salaries did not rise much in the nineties. Indeed, efficiency gains and corporate restructuring may have reduced the burden of salary costs for many companies. It may have appeared to the world that the country had a virtually infinite supply of white-collar workers. There was talk of how India's middle-class would do to global services trade what China had done to bulk manufacturing—Thomas Friedman's 'The Earth is Flat' hypothesis.

However, as the white-collar boom continued, the job market began to use up the slack. By 2004, there were palpable human-capital shortages in the high-growth sectors—for financial analysts, pilots, and IT project managers. However, soon the phenomenon spread to the middle class as a whole. Medical doctors began to leave the once sought-after government hospitals to join the new private hospitals or set up independent practice. The Minister of Health was quoted in a magazine saying that 'We're worried sick about the high rate of attrition from government hospitals.'[4] Similar concerns were being voiced by the armed forces which saw a sharp decline in the quality of officer-grade applicants. The Great Indian Middle Class was not so large after all!

Not surprisingly, salaries began to rise rapidly—first in the upper echelons but rapidly cascading down. By 2007, it was possible for those in senior managerial positions in successful companies to demand international-level salaries. The middle class had come a long way from the days when it was shocked at an annual salary of US$13,300—it was now commonplace for fresh MBA graduates from top schools to get multiples of that amount. In my own experience, the starting salaries of new recruits into the financial sector went up four-fold between 2000 and 2006. Surveys by Mercer Human Resources Consulting and Hewitt Associates showed that Indians were enjoying the highest salary increases in the world.

The rise in salaries meant that for the first time there was a palpable flow of expatriate Indians returning home. These returnees were not coming home just because of emotional attachments but because they were drawn by growing opportunities and rising salaries. Adjusted for purchasing power, senior managers in India are now the best paid in the world according to a list published by *The Economist*.[5] There are even press reports of how Indian doctors are leaving once sought-after jobs in Britain's National Health Service and going back to work in brand-new private hospitals. The doctors were cited saying that these hospitals paid better and had better equipment than the NHS.[6] Some Indian companies were now reporting a rise in applications even from skilled non-Indians who want to gain experience in this booming market. This is an amazing turnaround for a country that had only bled talent till now.

A tightening job market did not just cause a sharp increase in salaries. Employee turnover went up dramatically. Not so long ago, the middle-class worker took up his public-sector job and held it for the rest of his life. When the first call-centres were built in the late-nineties, one of the important advantages cited in favour of Indians was that they considered call-centre work as a career rather than a stopgap between other jobs. However, things have already changed and many sectors are now seeing turnover levels that are not much better than in the West. Employers have responded by digging deeper. Recruitment agents have spread out into the smaller towns and lesser-known universities. However, most employers would now agree that this could not go on much longer without making serious compromises on the quality of human capital. Gone are the days when one could hire a top-class IIT graduate for a pittance and make him/her work twelve hours a day.

The boom in salaries and rising turnover raises a serious question about India's unique growth model. India's white-collar trajectory was based on the easy availability of cheap, educated workers. Till recently, most observers had simply assumed that the country had an inexhaustible supply of white-collar workers. This was partly conditioned by the thought that a country with a billion people cannot possibly suffer from a tight labour-market. However, given the skewed education system, the billion people are not all capable of doing white-collar jobs and the effective workforce is far smaller. India is not the only place with this problem. Even China is suffering from serious shortages of managers and skilled workers. The difference is that China's growth model is not driven by the white-collar class but by the deployment of bulk labour. Thus, this particular problem does not fundamentally undermine the growth model in China.

How Big is the Middle Class?

If the country is already running out of middle-class workers, it raises the question—exactly how large is India's educated middle class? The number that is often quoted in the press is in the 250 to 300 million range[7]—but it is more an opinion than a fact. There is no credible study that backs this estimate. Of course, estimating the size of the middle class is more difficult than may appear at first sight. The lazy way is to simply define the top 5 per cent by income of the population as rich and then take the next 25–30 per cent of the population as the middle class (which is what appears to have been done in the above case). However, this is a meaningless number since all societies will have a 'middle class' by this definition, even a Neolithic village. Therefore, the middle class has to be defined against an absolute income threshold rather than on a relative basis. This too is not easy because any absolute income bracket is necessarily arbitrary and may not be comparable across time and place.

The alternative methodology of defining the middle class in terms of consumption rather than income does not solve the problem. A consumption basket that may be considered middle class at one time may not be so in another time. Take for instance the use of mobile phones. In the mid-nineties, mobile phones were used only by the rich. By the end of the decade, it was common enough amongst the middle class. Now its use has grown far beyond the middle class. Most difficult of all is the problem that the middle class is best understood in terms of its social values and attitudes (for instance, its emphasis on higher education). These are subjective attributes and just as difficult to define and measure.

Despite all these problems, a few researchers have attempted to define and study this group systematically. A study by McKinsey's Global Institute published in May 2007 defined the middle class as those with incomes between US$4,400 and US$22,000 per annum.[8] Although this is low by global standards, this is equivalent to US$23,500 and US$118,000 in Purchasing Power Parity terms and purchases a recognizable middle-class lifestyle. The study found that the current size of the middle class is just 50 million (or 13 million households). This is a fraction of the commonly used estimate and an even smaller fraction of the total population.

The above estimate fits very well with other measurable attributes of the middle class. Since everyone is so excited about the 'educated' middle class, let's look at the stock of manpower with tertiary education. According to the estimates of the Institute of Applied Manpower Research in New Delhi,[9] the stock of manpower with higher education in 2001 was as follows: 0.41 million with degrees in medicine/dentistry, 0.3 million with degrees in agricultural/veterinary sciences, 12.7 million with degrees in the Arts/Social Sciences, 5.7 million with Commerce degrees, 4.8 million with Science degrees and finally 2.5 million engineers. That is a grand total of 26.4 million. Even if one ignores the uneven quality of this group, the fact remains that India's middle class was not very large at the turn of the century. Even allowing for subsequent growth, it is difficult to justify a number that is significantly larger than the McKinsey estimate of 50 million.

Note that I not trying to provide an exact estimate of the size of this social group. I am merely pointing out that the usually quoted number of 300 million is a gross overestimate of the middle class's capability to feed the existing Indian growth model. This fits with what we are now observing in the white-collar job market. If this class was indeed 300 million strong, it is very unlikely that the country would be seeing the fastest salary growth in the world. It is better to think in terms of a small but underemployed middle-class in the early nineties that is now somewhat larger but fully employed.

The smaller-than-anticipated pool of white-collar workers poses a serious problem for the current economic trajectory with its emphasis on high-skill activities. Information technology and telecommunications will not make the world flat for those who do not have skills to participate in globalization. I am not saying that all Indian IT and ITES companies will shortly grind to a halt. Some of them will be able to deal with higher employee costs because they now have the capacity to innovate up the value chain.

However, it must be recognized that it is much more difficult to generate GDP growth of more than 8 per cent per year through continuous productivity improvements than through simple wage-arbitrage. The size of the middle-class is, of course, growing. However, as we will see, the tertiary education system is not growing the skills base fast enough to meet the demand. Quality-adjusted data is not available but recent experience with corporate recruitment suggests that the shortages are escalating at an exponential rate. Many international commentators have begun to question the Indian model. A *Financial Times* article in December 2007 read, 'a longer term shift in strategy is necessary if India's IT companies are to prevent more work going overseas . . .'[10]

So, is this the end of the Indian dream run? Is there an alternative growth path that does not rely exclusively on the educated middle-class? Are there ways in which the middle class itself can be made to grow faster? Fortunately, there are reasons to be optimistic on all these counts. In later chapters we will look at powerful long-term dynamics that could give the Indian economy a completely different, new growth dynamic. But first, let us look at how the entrepreneurial explosion and the middle-class-driven growth path affected the vast majority of Indians—the poor.

5

Poverty, Inequality and the Last Bastion of Control

The entrepreneurial explosion and the middle-class-driven growth dynamic came into full bloom after 2003. Between 2003 and 2007, GDP expanded at a pace of almost 9 per cent per annum. Growth led to spiralling stock markets and real-estate prices. A lot of people became very rich overnight. Indian billionaires grinned on the covers of international business magazines and the new breed of Indian multinationals bought global brands. However, was there a decline in poverty and an improvement in the lot of the average Indian? This is very important for a poor country like India. Thus, before we look to the future, it is necessary to look at what has happened to poverty and employment since 1991.

There are many people who still argue that liberalization and globalization have not made a meaningful dent on poverty and that things may have become worse because employment opportunities for the poor have declined since 1991. In other words, they argue that the post-liberalization acceleration in growth benefitted only the educated middle-class that participated in the services boom and that the gains did not trickle down to the vast majority. They will inevitably point to the teeming slums of Mumbai as proof. Unfortunately, such finger-pointing does not tell us much because there were plenty of slums in pre-liberalization India. No one doubts that there is still a lot of poverty in India. What we need to gauge is whether or not the poverty situation is becoming better or worse.

The Debate over Poverty and Jobless Growth

In order to investigate this allegation, let us first consider the statistics. According to the National Sample Survey (NSS) data, the proportion of the population that lived below the poverty line stood at 51.3 per cent in 1977-78. This ratio declined through the eighties as growth accelerated and by 1993-94 it stood at 37.3 per cent. This decline in poverty is generally accepted. So far so good. Then came the liberalization of the nineties—inefficient subsidies were rolled back, industries were deregulated and the public sector was forced to reform. As the bloated public and private industrial units tried to boost productivity, there was a sharp decline in hiring even as thousands were laid off (especially through voluntary retirement schemes). Jobs were being created during this time in the middle-class-driven services sector but these were presumably white-collar jobs and therefore few in number. There was a presumption amongst the Left-leaning critics of liberalization that the goal of poverty removal had been abandoned in favour of efficiency and profits. Many outraged academics published articles in learned journals about the dangers of 'jobless growth'.

Therefore, it came as a shock to them when the NSS surveys of 1999-2000 showed that the proportion of population living below the poverty line had declined sharply to 26 per cent. The level of poverty had not only declined but the rate of poverty reduction had accelerated! The finding triggered a furious debate about the veracity of the statistics. Economists from the Left argued that the NSS had grossly under-reported poverty. They questioned the statistics and the survey methodology. Economists from the Right responded by suggesting that the survey had actually over-reported poverty levels.

The 'Great Indian Poverty Debate' had less to do with statistics and more to do with ideologies. I will spare the readers the arcane details of the controversy over whether or not the NSS should have used a seven-day recall period or a thirty-day recall period. Those who are interested in the intricacies of this dispute are referred to the writings of Angus Deaton and Valerie Kozel.[1] The whole issue was finally put to rest with the publication of NSS data for 2004-05. The share of population below the poverty line had declined further of 22 per cent! This is still a very high level of poverty but, there could be no doubt that free markets had done a far better job at reducing absolute poverty than all the 'scientific' input-output models of Mahalanobis. Best of all, the data showed that poverty declines had been faster in rural areas than in the cities.

The latest data may have proved that faster growth has indeed led to absolute declines in poverty but it does not explain how this was achieved when employment growth was so slow in the late nineties. Employment growth was 1.2 per cent per year in the nineties compared to 2.5 per cent in the eighties. Even more puzzling is the finding that this slowdown in job creation did not cause a discernable increase in inequality or in unemployment rates. Most puzzling of all, why did real wages accelerate from 2.4 per cent per annum in the eighties to 4.4 per cent in the nineties. This cannot be explained by biases created by the expansion of urban white-collar jobs because rural wages also accelerated.

A study by Surjit Bhalla and Tirthamoy Das holds part of the answer.[2] They argue that contrary to widely held beliefs, the size of country's available workforce grew at a slower pace in the nineties than during the eighties. This was due to the increases in school enrollment rates during the nineties, something we will revisit later in this book. As enrollment rates rose, there was a decline in participation by child labour (i.e. those below 15 years) as well as those on the 15–24 years age bracket. Lower participation by the young meant that the available workforce expanded at a slower pace and, in turn, this forced up wages despite slower employment generation. This is corroborated by OECD estimates that show that labour force growth slowed from 2.2 per cent per year during 1983–93 to 0.6 per cent during 1994–2000.[3] In other words, the primary education enrollments not only increased literacy rates but averted an increase in unemployment during the difficult period of industrial restructuring. However, this still begs the question—how did a services-driven growth path cause poverty to decline so rapidly in rural India?

Liberalization and Rural India

Seventy per cent of Indians still live in villages and farming provides full or part-time employment to 55 per cent of the workforce. This does not mean that things are not changing. Most middle-class city dwellers have an idealized view of village life—an existence dominated by the cycle of agriculture, touched perhaps by the Green Revolution of the sixties and seventies, but otherwise unchanging and eternal. This image is reinforced by patronizing reports that appear in the media and in the pages of learned journals. The reality is quite different. Things may have changed little in some remote areas but for the vast majority of villages, the transformation is more than visible—mobile telephones, television, cinema, literacy and migrant workers have all caused palpable changes in ideas, aspirations and lifestyles.

First of all, we need to revisit the idea that the rural economy is solely about farming. In fact, the share of agriculture has been declining rapidly as a driver of not just the overall economy but even of the rural economy. The farm sector accounted for barely 17 per cent of GDP in 2007 compared to around 32 per cent in 1991. In a series of studies, Andrew Foster and Mark Rosenzweig[4] found that in the three decades between 1970 and 2000, growth in non-farm incomes was substantial and that the primary source of this growth was rural industry. Their data suggests that non-farm employee incomes accounted for 40 per cent of total rural incomes and that the impact of rural factories on real wages was twice that of agricultural productivity gains from the Green Revolution. Significantly, they found that expansion in rural industry was not predicated on increases in local agricultural productivity (if anything, it was affected negatively by wage increases). Most interesting of all, they found that non-farm growth reduced inequality in the rural areas in contrast to agricultural growth which benefitted the larger land-owners. In short, rapid growth in the non-farm activities was simultaneously increasing incomes and reducing inequality in rural areas.

The data for these studies end in the late nineties. However, even a casual observer can tell that the process has accelerated into the new century with improvements in telecommunications and spreading education. In particular, there has been a significant jump in non-farm services—cable television, local taxis, motorcycle repair shops and so on. Many of the existing service-providers have upgraded themselves to take advantage of changing aspirations. The village barber who once operated under a tree has built a 'Hair cutting Saloon' or even a 'Beauty Parlour'. The village tea-shop, that till recently functioned out of a shack built of bamboo, is now a 'Hotel' that serves 'Dosa/Samosa/Chinese—100% Pure Veg'. All this may not appear especially sophisticated to the city-slicker but it is a quantum shift.

But what about agriculture? Although it is losing its monopoly over the rural economy, it is still a very important source of income and employment. The sector averages a growth rate of almost 3 per cent per year which is adequate to feed the country's growing population but not enough to provide a real boost to the rural economy. Furthermore, it remains vulnerable to variations in the weather. Not so long ago the stock market rose and fell in line with the quantity and distribution of the annual monsoon rains. The rest of the economy has moved on but the agricultural sector remains very volatile. This leaves a large population of small, marginal farmers very vulnerable. Every year, there are media reports from some part of the country where farmers have committed suicide following crop failure.

This problem has not persisted because of the lack of public spending. Both the Central and the state governments continue to spend large amounts on various kinds of subsidies. The real problem is that these are very poorly targeted, and often worsen the problem. Take for example, the electricity subsidy—farmers in many states are given cheap or even free power. The idea is that this will help farmers irrigate their fields by pumping ground water during droughts. Unfortunately, this only helps those who can dig deep tube-wells and install powerful pumps (i.e. the rich farmers). In contrast, the poor farmer finds that the water-table drops year after year and is eventually out of reach for their traditional wells. In some places, the water table falls so low that the village wells used for drinking water also dry up and the women have to walk for miles to get water for their homes.

Therefore, despite all the subsidies and the Green Revolution, productivity remains low and output volatile. One of the main problems is that this sector attracts very little investment—less than 10 per cent of overall investment (the subsidies are mostly oriented to consumables like electricity and fertilizer). The reason for this is that agriculture is the one major sector that was not meaningfully liberalized in the nineties. Even today the sector suffers from a plethora of restrictions on internal and external trade, wasteful state-run procurement systems, and all kinds of restrictions on the entry of private corporate players. This leads to huge inefficiencies in the sector. For instance, a government subsidy/support price may end up encouraging too much production of a certain crop in one part of the country. This is then purchased by the state-run procurement system that is not capable of either storing it or selling it, and eventually wastes this surplus. Meanwhile, there may serious shortages in other crops and in other parts of the country. The burden of this system is so large that economists Rip Landes and Ashok Gulati feel that the agricultural sector as a whole was effectively heavily taxed through the eighties and nineties (even after accounting for the subsidies).[5]

Despite all these problems, liberalization and openness are leading to major changes even in the agricultural sector. Perhaps the most important agent of change has been the expansion in telecommunications. Till the eighties, telecommunications were a public-sector monopoly. Telephones were seen as an urban luxury and the service was unreliable. Even in cities like Delhi, it took a great deal of effort, sometimes bribery, to get a connection. In the villages, telephones were virtually unknown and 97 per cent of the country's 600,000 villages had no telephone at all.[6] The thinking of the pre-liberalization planners was that the villages needed pesticides and fertilizers, not telephones. After all, so the argument went, what would illiterate farmers do with a telephone?

It was into this milieu that Sam Pitroda arrived from the US. Born in a remote village in Orissa in 1942, he had emigrated to the US in the mid-sixties. By 1980, he had built up a very successful telecommunications business in Chicago. In the early eighties, he came up with the then-radical vision that the land of his birth could be transformed by introducing state-of-the-art telecommunications to the rural areas. This flew in the face of the received wisdom of the time but, after a great deal of persistence, he managed to convince Rajiv Gandhi of his idea. When Rajiv Gandhi became Prime Minister in late 1984, Sam Pitroda got his opportunity. With the Prime Minister's personal support, he set about upgrading the country's communications system. Most importantly, he began to push for rural exchanges.

This first attempt to introduce rural telephony faced many technological and political challenges. Both Sam Pitroda and his project came under attack from many quarters, especially after Rajiv Gandhi was defeated in the 1989 elections. However, the central idea survived and through the early nineties 'Public Call Operators' or PCOs appeared in many rural areas. These were nothing more than public phones run by shopkeepers but they proved immensely popular. It turned out that those illiterate farmers really did want to talk to other people—to find out prices of farm produce in the next town, to ask for help in an emergency, to talk to relatives who had migrated to the city.

What then turned this process into a revolution was the liberalization of the telecommications sector and the entry of private cellular operators. The availability of cheap and reliable mobile telephones created a whole new world of opportunities for rural areas. Take the example of how the fishing industry was transformed in the state of Kerala. Fishing is a very important part of the economy of this coastal state but it suffered from a major inefficiency. The prices varied very sharply between different ports depending on the daily supply and demand situation. A survey of prices in the Kasaragod district between 7.45 a.m. and 8.00 a.m. on 14 January 1997 showed that a kilogram of sardines sold for Rs 9.70 in Thaikadappuram and at Rs 4 at Aarikkadi. In the beach market of Kasaba there were no buyers that day and the price was effectively zero. These are all located within the same district and are just a few miles apart along the coast, but the lack of market information resulted in serious inefficiency and wastage.

From 1997, mobile telephony began to spread across Kerala. The fishermen soon discovered that many of the base towers were close enough to the shore and that the service was available up to twenty-five kilometres out at sea. It did not take them long to use their phones while still at sea to compare prices across different fish markets along the coast. This meant that the fisherman could change course and take his catch to the best market for that day. The result was dramatic decline in price variation along the Kerala coast. The fishermen's profits rose even as the consumer cost declined, not to mention the overall decline in market uncertainty.[7] In other words, improvements in systemic efficiency allowed the same level of output to provide a significantly higher income. This is but a single illustration of how rural India has been transformed by the power of free enterprise.

Inequality and Unemployability

We know now that liberalization is doing well in terms of reducing absolute poverty. Deprivation still affects large sections of the population but we are generally on the right track. Nonetheless, the current set-up does have one unwelcome side-effect—the rise of relative inequality. The economic boom clearly created white-collar jobs and increased middle-class salaries. Unfortunately, not everyone could fully participate in the skills-driven growth model. The poor—including those in rural areas—have benefitted indirectly from trickle down and from improvements in systemic efficiency. The story of the Kerala fishermen is an example. This was good enough to push down absolute poverty but the gains have disproportionately benefitted the middle-class and the business community.

This has led to the growing gap of a very peculiar kind—not so much the gap between the employed and the unemployed as had been the case in pre-liberalization era. The unique Indian growth model is generating plenty of well-paying jobs but in many cases only the educated middle-class has the skills to take advantage of them. Since this group is now fully deployed, its salaries are spiralling out. Thus, there is a growing gap between the employed and the unemployable, the skilled and the unskilled. This is not just a problem for income inequality but also for sustaining the existing skills-dependent growth model. For a country with more than a billion people, why are more people unable to join the middle-class?

The skilled middle class will grow naturally over time as the economy expands but this process will require ever-growing numbers to develop the capabilities needed to take advantage of the opportunities. In other words, the first requirement for sustaining the current growth model is expansion in tertiary education. Higher education is key to social and economic mobility. With the spread of primary and secondary education, ever larger numbers will enter the workforce over the next decade with some basic education. The vast majority of these people will come from humble backgrounds. Good quality tertiary education is their best passport into the middle class. This is a win-win situation for all—the country gets a larger middle class in order to feed its growth engine while the individual gets to climb the social ladder.

On the other hand, if the gates are not opened wide enough, a large proportion of the aspirants will not be able to take the next step. This is not just a waste of talent but it could lead to social tensions. Given the age profile of the population, it is almost certain that over the next decade the competition for higher education will become ever more fierce. Things have perhaps already gone too far. Take my own college for instance. Shri Ram College of Commerce is arguably one of the best institutions in the country for studying commerce and economics. However, prospective students now need to score a minimum of 95 per cent in their secondary school examinations to have any hope of entering this institution. This is ten percentage points higher than the minimum requirement in the late eighties. The increasingly bitter debate over caste-based quotas and affirmative action is the result of this scarcity problem.

It should be clear that instead of frustrating the growing demand for higher education (and risking social tensions), this pressure should be accommodated through a massive supply response. Unfortunately, the system is not just unable to expand fast but is unable to service even the existing network. Oddly, there is widely held view that India's higher education system is very good. In May 2005, an article in *Business Week* concluded that 'unlike China, India's significant cheap labour is not a pool of factory workers, but a huge crop of scientists'.[8] This impression has been created by the success of India's white-collar professionals at home and abroad. It is entirely fiction.

It is true that socialist-era India ignored primary education at the expense of tertiary education. This led to the creation of a highly educated middle-class amidst a mass of illiterates. However, this view is now increasingly outdated. We will see in the next chapter how the combined efforts of the government, NGOs, individuals and, more recently, private fee-paying schools have changed the supply dynamics of primary and secondary education since the late nineties. These improvements have created a pipeline of students wanting to enter higher education, feeding, in turn, the pool of skilled workers.

Yet, the pool of highly skilled workers remains small. Little more than 30 million Indians have graduate degrees, hardly an unlimited supply and certainly nowhere near the 300 million middle-class that is often touted. Even more worryingly, quality is a serious problem. The success of a few elite institutions has hidden the poor standards of the wider system. This is why we are seeing such large jumps in white-collar salaries in a country with such a large population.

Fortunately, the educated middle class can be made to grow. Today's Indian middle class was the result of two previous shifts in tertiary education—first, in the mid-nineteenth century (as a result of Ram Mohan Roy's efforts) and then one in the mid-twentieth century (as a result of the first burst of public-sector investment). By sharply expanding the provision of quality higher education, we could now further expand the middle-class. There is now a pipeline of working-class students coming up the primary/secondary education system who want to enter the middle class and enjoy the high salaries of white-collar workers. Why not take advantage of this demand for tertiary education by opening out the gates?

A Brief History of Higher Education in India

India has a long and venerable history in the field of higher education. In ancient times, the country was home to perhaps the oldest formal universities in the world. The more important of these ancient universities were Takshila (now in Pakistan), Nalanda (in the modern state of Bihar) and Ujjaini (in modern Madhya Pradesh). These were famous in the ancient world and attracted students from all parts of India, Central Asia, China and South-east Asia. The Hindu-Buddhist university of Takshila, the oldest, was probably established in the sixth century BC. Unfortunately, Takshila university were destroyed by the White Huns (Ephthalites) around 460 AD. In 1193, Nalanda was sacked and totally destroyed by Bakhtiyar Khilji. This event not only ended the university but was also followed by a rapid decline in the practise of Buddhism in India. In 1235, Sultan Iltutmish completely destroyed Ujjaini—a major centre for mathematics, literature, philosophy and astronomy. It is significant that at exactly the same time, half-way across the world, Oxford University was being established.

The following centuries saw a few centres of Islamic and Hindu learning emerge. However, India would not produce another world-class university for several hundred years. It was only during British colonial rule that formal university education was revived. Modern colleges were set up in Agra, Nagpur, Calcutta, Bombay and Madras in the early nineteenth century. This introduction of Western knowledge, made accessible through the knowledge of English, was a very important factor that allowed the emergence of India's middle class. In 1857, three federal examining universities on the pattern of London University were established in the three main British-controlled cities of Calcutta, Bombay and Madras.[9] The existing colleges were affiliated to these universities. Over the next several decades, more universities were created and by 1947 there were 25 universities in the country.

After Independence, higher education went through rapid expansion. The number of universities in the country jumped from 25 in 1947 to 348 in 2005.[10] Enrollment rose from 0.1 million in 1947 to 10.5 million in 2005. This may appear at first sight to be a major success but the numbers are misleading. There are serious problems with quality when one looks beyond the handful of elite institutions like the IIMs, the IITs and Delhi University. The level of research even in the elite universities has steadily deteriorated over the years. Few of the best students stay back after graduation—many leaving the country for universities in the West. This is why the country is suddenly suffering from serious shortages in skilled manpower. In short, India's tertiary education system is in no position to take on the challenge of supporting a dynamic economic engine.

The Problem with Higher Education

The country's higher education institutions have an enrolment of 10.5 million students and turn out 2.5 million each year. About 45 per cent of the students pursue degrees in the arts, 20 per cent in sciences and 18 per cent in commerce. The remaining 17 per cent are enrolled in professional courses like law and medicine. The sheer numbers may seem large but remember that it is small for a country of India's size. China, for instance, has an enrollment level of 24 million—and that country does not rely on the educated middle class as the primary source of growth.

Besides, the popular press often quotes numbers that

massively exaggerate both Indian and Chinese numbers. For instance, the number of engineers being produced by the US every year is often put at 70,000 while the numbers for China and India are put at 600,000 and 350,000 respectively. However, this statistic is grossly inaccurate as it compares apples with mangoes and bamboo shoots because it ignores many US institutions while for the Asians it includes all kinds of diplomas and certificates. According to a study by Gary Gereffi and Vivek Wadhwa of Duke University, when one compares like to like (i.e. proper engineering degrees), the numbers look as follows: 137,000 for the United States, 351,000 for China and 112,000 for India.[11]

More worrying than the numbers, however, is the quality problem. Even some of the colleges affiliated to elite universities have limited facilities, truant lecturers and irregular classes. Matters deteriorate rapidly when one is dealing with lesser-known colleges and institutions. In many cases syllabuses have not been updated for three or four decades and many of the prescribed textbooks are out of print. Economics courses in parts of the country still teach their students about the joys of the Mahalanobis model of development, fifteen years after liberalization. Courses taught in Indian languages suffer from serious limitations due to the unavailability of translated course materials. To add to this, the examination system is both outdated and unreliable. In recent years, there has been a spate of scandals over how examination questions were leaked by unscrupulous officials.

The second quality-related problem with higher education is that it is limited by subject silos that are not oriented towards employability. In its cover story on 7 March 2005, *India Today* identified the following emerging job opportunities—hospitality, biotech, education & training, aviation, event management, fitness consultancy, and fashion design. Yet, the country has very few institutions to train students for these specialized careers. The academic establishment remains wedded to the obsolete idea that the education system should restrict itself to proving general rather than specific skills.

It is difficult to provide an objective measure of quality and employment-relevance of the higher education system as a whole. However, it is telling that 40 per cent of graduates are not productively employed in a country that is suffering from rapidly rising white-collar salaries and severe skill shortages.[12] The fact that they are not being sucked in by the job market suggests that they are considered unemployable. A McKinsey study in 2005 concluded that only 25 per cent of Indian-trained engineers and 15 per cent of finance/accounting professionals have the skills to work for an international company. Just 10 per cent of graduates with generalist degrees in arts and humanities made the grade.[13]

The third problem is the inability of universities to retain graduates for higher degrees and for research. For instance, India produces 6,000 doctorates per year compared to 25,000 by US universities. About 4 per cent of US science/engineering graduates and 7 per cent of those in Europe finish their doctorates. The rate for India is not even 0.4 per cent. Moreover the numbers are growing very slowly. In contrast, China produced barely a thousand doctorates in 1990 but now produces over 9,000 per year—and the number is rising rapidly.

Some apologists may be tempted to argue that the number of doctorates is low because of stringent quality control. The evidence is entirely to the contrary. The Verma Committee enquiring into the status of higher education in Bihar found that a single thesis was used successfully by as many as eight students to gain a PhD![14]

The poor quality of post-graduate education has resulted in a serious outflow of the best students to Western universities. An estimated 100,000 Indian students go abroad every year to study in universities in the Unites States and Britain, and more recently in Australia, New Zealand and Singapore. They spend around US$5 billion in tuition fees and living expenses. Till very recently, few returned. Of about 140,000 graduates of the Indian Institutes of Technology, it is estimated that around 40,000 have emigrated to the US alone. According to Sanat Kaul, they have been responsible for creating 150,000 jobs and US$80 billion worth of market capitalization in their host country.[15] In other words, the poor quality of higher education is not just failing to provide relevant skills but is actively encouraging brain drain and costing a lot of money.

Given this deterioration in the quality of postgraduate education and research, no Indian resident has won the Nobel Prize since Independence. Several Indians have won the prestigious award since Independence—Hargobind Khorana (1968, Medicine), S. Chandrashekar (1983, Physics) and Amartya Sen (1998, Economics). Yet all of them spent their working lives in foreign universities. Indeed, not a single resident Indian has been even been a serious contender for the Nobel Prize in recent decades.[16] Yet, Indians like C.V. Raman (1930, Physics) and Rabindranath Tagore (1913, Literature) had been able to overcome all kinds of hurdles and prejudices to win the prize while the country was still under British rule.

The Last Bastion of State Control

The most striking feature of the current tertiary education bottleneck is the similarity with the scarcities that plagued most goods and services in the pre-liberalization era. During the socialist years, government licensing created queues and waitlists for everything ranging from telephones to cars. Quality was usually poor because there was no competition in the resulting sellers' market. However, it should not be surprising that the same scarcity and quality problems today plague the university system because it is one of the last remnants of the government license-regime. What makes it worse is that the government and academic establishment has a deep-seated prejudice that the higher education should not be oriented towards the economic needs of the country. Pavan Agarwal sums up in his paper this line of thinking: 'There is near unanimity about the fact that the economic role of higher education is not its primary role.'

Government control over higher education is effected through multiple agencies and a complex web of rules and regulations. According to the Constitution, education is in the Concurrent List which means that both the state and Central government have a say in how this sector is run. Therefore, both the state and central education departments[17] and agencies play a role. The University Grants Commission (UGC) is the apex national body for the university system. Its mandate is one of co-ordination and maintenance of standards. As the name suggests, the UGC releases funds for universities but it also devises common pay scales, and confers recognition to universities.

Then there are thirteen professional councils at the national level. These include bodies such as the Medical Council of India, the Council of Architects, the National Council for Agricultural Research, the Bar Council of India and so on. As if this were not enough, there are also state-level professional councils. At every stage, there is a great deal of overlap between the state and Central education departments, the UGC, the national professional councils and the state professional councils. For instance, the work of the All India Council for Technical Education overlaps with that of the

UGC, the Distance Education Councils, the Council of Architects, the Pharmacy Council of India and the State Councils for Technical Education.[18] All this creates an extremely confusing web of regulations and institutional egos that educational institutions have to carefully navigate.

Over-regulation is made worse by the fact that there is dwindling public funding for the sector. The current design of the tertiary-education sector makes the sector reliant on public financing. However, estimates for financial year 2004-05 indicate that the Central and state governments spent only Rs 131.4 billion (or US$3 billion). This is barely 0.4 per cent of GDP and this share has been declining since the early eighties even as the number of students has been rising. According to Tilak,[19] this has meant that between 1991 and 2003 there was a 28 per cent decline in spending per student. As a result India spends barely US$400 per student compared to US$2,730 for China and an average of US$10,000 for developed countries. It is therefore not surprising that quality has suffered.

Part of the solution, therefore, must be to increase financing for the sector. However, despite the promises, the government's finances are in no position to increase support on a sustained basis. Since public financing cannot be increased to the necessary scale, the obvious alternative is to increase private financing—especially through increases in fees. Unfortunately, this is such a political hot potato that fees are ludicrously low for many institutions. Cost recovery through fees is lower than 10 per cent in elite institutions such as Delhi University and Jawaharlal Nehru University, Delhi. Even though there have been some increases in fees in the last few years, the available money is barely enough to meet running costs and certainly not enough to fund new universities and attract teaching talent. This is sad for a country that is spending US$5 billion every year to send its best students abroad.

So what is the solution? In my view, we need to apply the same principles to education as was applied to the rest of the economy—open the sector to the private sector and to foreign parties. This will increase both supply and quality, and at the same time force efficiency gains that would lower the cost of delivery. Even the existing public-sector universities would benefit from the competition just as public-sector banks gained from liberalization of the banking sector.

Unfortunately, the academic establishment has been strongly opposed to such a market-driven solution. There are two main lines of argument. First, it is argued that education is a 'public good' since the expansion in education has general benefits to society that go beyond the 'private good' of the individual student. This implies that the individual student would invest less in education than is socially optimal. Therefore, the argument goes, education cannot be left to the vagaries and whims of the market. Second, it is argued that private companies would look to maximize profits and not quality. This would lead to high fees and low standards.

Both arguments do not stand to scrutiny although they have been used in other countries as well. However, in India these arguments have been taken to an extreme and, as we have seen, caused serious damage.[20] First, let us take the argument that the social benefits from education are so high that we will get socially 'optimal' investment only if the government intervenes in the sector. It is true that education has general social benefits but this misses the point that education is mostly a private good that provides huge advantages to the individual. As the well-known economist Ajay Shah puts it—'I study. I benefit'.[21] Therefore, it is totally absurd to argue that the State should intervene because Indians would not invest in education unless it was heavily subsidized. As we will see in the next chapter, the very poorest Indians are willing to invest in private-school education for their children. Indeed, they clearly prefer to pay fees for a good education over free but poor-quality government education. It is true that things will be difficult for some of the poorer students in a purely fee-paying university system but the answer is to find financing solutions such as scholarships and loans. The point is that even the poor do not want cheap but sub-standard universities.

The second argument is that a market-driven education system would maximize revenues but not quality. Again, this is no more tenable that saying than an automobiles sector must be nationalized because car manufacturers maximize profits. Reputation and quality matter, and private universities will only be able to demand a premium if they provide a good service. It is true that reputations take time to establish and, in a rapidly expanding system, some private players may indeed try to 'cheat'. The recent experience in the state of Chhattisgarh illustrates this problem. In 2002, the state legislature passed the Chhattisgarh Private Universities Act. Within a year the state saw the establishment of 112 universities. Some of them were genuine establishments, but many were 'cash-for-degrees' operations without buildings or teaching staff. Eventually, in February 2005, the Supreme Court banned these universities. The status of the 50,000 students enrolled in these institutions still remains unclear.

This experience is often used by the anti-liberalization academic establishment as an example of what would happen if the private sector were allowed to enter the sector. Again, this is a specious argument. Liberalization does not mean chaos. This is a problem of governance that plagues many sectors—including many where the private sector is doing very well. All it takes is to create a neutral regulator that establishes and enforces standards (in the same way the Telecom Regulatory

Authority maintains order in the telecommunications sector). The UGC could well play this role but its focus and powers will have to be radically altered.[22] It could not be an effective referee if the academic establishment maintains its attitude that private-sector involvement, especially that of foreign universities, is essentially bad.

Meanwhile, despite all the hurdles, private institutions have been entering the tertiary-education sector. Perhaps the most visible manifestation of this phenomenon is the growth of private institutes that cater for specialized segments that are not covered by the mainstream universities. The most well-known example of this phenomenon is the National Institute of Information Technology (NIIT).

Despite the rather public-sector name, NIIT is a purely private network of training centres that brought computer education to India. It was set up in 1981 by Rajendra Pawar and Vijay Thadani and by the early nineties it had a branch in virtually every urban centre in the country. It became commonplace for university and high-school students to do IT courses in the evenings. It is said that the company single-handedly trained one-third of the country's software professionals. Today NIIT has operations in thirty countries across the world. Without NIIT and other such private efforts, India's software revolution would not have taken off. Even after years of rapid expansion, skill shortages in the software sector are far less problematic than in less successful sectors.

The success of NIIT (and other such enterprises) has important lessons for how the private sector can be used to rapidly grow tertiary education across the country within a very short period. After all, the NIIT experiment is not unique—we have already seen how the liberalized private sector was able to affect explosive expansions in cable television, civil aviation and in mobile telephony. As a market-driven system, a private sector cannot only expand fast but would also respond automatically to the changing demands for skills. Moreover, competition and efficiency gains are likely to drive down the cost per student for providing this education. The privately run Manipal Institute of Technology, for instance, spends less than half the amount spent by the State-run IITs on each student.

Elements within the academic establishment and the political elite still remain strongly opposed to liberalizing the education sector. The Foreign Education Providers Bill that would have allowed entry of foreign universities was stalled by the Communists in 2007. It does not matter whether this is a case of misplaced ideology or a cynical attempt to retain control for personal benefit. The point is that tertiary education is a major bottleneck for the economy and the problem must be eased as soon as possible. Failure to resolve this problem not only endangers the current skill-hungry growth model but is also the leading cause of growing inequality.

Thankfully, the sheer weight of the problem may force change. Even as this book was being written, there was a growing chorus of voices demanding reform. The proliferation of unregulated 'institutes' in the smaller towns mirrors the stresses within the system. The National Knowledge Commission headed by the indomitable Sam Pitroda has been strongly recommending that the sector be liberalized and that its regulation be handed to an independent authority in order to replicate the successful use of independent regulators in sectors such as telecommunications. Even within the political elite, there are a many who now openly argue for liberalization.[23]

With each reform, higher education will expand and will feed the middle class. In turn, the middle class will demand more reform. Of course, all this will take several years to bear fruit. Meanwhile, will skill shortages cause the Indian growth engine to grind to a halt? Fortunately, the country is now about to benefit from two socio-economic shifts that will fundamentally change the growth dynamic in a way that will benefit a wider population as well as rely less on high-end skills. We now turn to these 'Two Revolutions'.

6

Two Revolutions

So far, India's unique economic model was the result of both positive and negative factors. On the positive side, there was the easy availability of cheap but educated middle-class workers. The globalizing technological shift in communications made it possible for these white-collar workers to quickly absorb new ideas as well as participate in the international marketplace. On the negative side, there was the high cost of capital reflecting relatively low savings rates and, as a consequence, low investment in physical infrastructure and manufacturing capacity. In addition, there was the problem of widespread illiteracy that rendered the bulk of the labour force unsuitable for all but the most basic subsistence farming. It was the combination of all these factors that had so far driven India's unique skill-driven economic trajectory.

However, the middle class cannot be expected to carry the rest of the economy on its own for much longer. As we have seen, it is no longer under-employed and is rapidly re-pricing itself. The fossilized tertiary education system is not capable of expanding the skill base fast enough. A growth model based exclusively on the existing middle-class, therefore, is increasingly untenable. Fortunately, India may be about to benefit from two major long-term shifts—one in its population dynamics, and one in primary education. The combination of these two factors will re-define India over the next twenty years.

The Demographic Revolution

India's large and growing population has long been seen as a problem, perhaps even the most important long-term problem facing the country. This is not surprising given the sustained increase in population in the second half of the twentieth century—from 361 million in 1951 to around 1.1 billion in 2007. Between 1951 and 1991, the country's population grew at an average rate of over 2 per cent per year. This was a serious problem for an economy growing at the Nehru–Mahalanobis rate of 3.5 per cent since there was very little left over for increasing standards of living. By the seventies, population control and family planning became a recognized part of government policy.

For the most part, the government campaign was aimed at increasing awareness about the use of contraceptives. Although there are allegations of forced sterilization during the Emergency years, India's efforts were not as coercive as the Chinese 'One Child Policy'. Nonetheless, birth rates did begin to decline in the eighties from 34 per thousand in 1981 to 25 two decades later. It does not matter whether this was due to government family planning efforts or because of the spread of literacy and modern medicine, the point is that this allowed the rate of population growth to drift down to 1.6 per cent by 2005 (with the promise that it would decline steadily in future).

This phenomenon of acceleration and subsequent deceleration in population growth has very important economic implications but it is hardly unique to India. The nineteenth and twentieth centuries saw major demographic shifts around the world—beginning with Western Europe and then spreading to other parts of the world. As modern medicine and food habits spread, death rates declined rapidly. Initially birth rates did not fall along with death rates. The gap between death and birth rates caused a sharp acceleration in the pace of population growth. After a while, however, birth rates also decline sharply as social attitudes change and contraceptives become more easily available. Population growth rates slowed and the average age rose. We have seen this happen in country after country.

Note how the time lag between the declines in death and birth rates causes a bulge in the age structure that works its way through the population over time. On a stylized account, the population then witnesses three stages of demographic transition:

— In the first stage, there is an increase in the proportion of the young in the population as birth rates stay high but infant mortality declines. There are lots of children but relatively few old people.

— In the second stage, the proportion of children declines as birth rates decline and that of the old increases modestly as people live longer. However, most importantly, the share of working-age adults increases sharply as the population bulge enters its prime years.

— In the third stage, the proportions of the young and working-age adults fall while that of old people rises.

Virtually every major country and region has witnessed demographic change in the last century, but different areas are in different phases of transition. Western Europe was the first to witness the introduction of modern medicine and changes in social attitudes. The process appears to have started in late eighteenth-century France but spread to newly industrializing Britain and then to across the rest of Western Europe. It was a gradual process that took several decades to spread. Nonetheless, it did cause a population explosion in nineteenth-century Europe that fed mass immigration to colonies in the Americas and elsewhere. According to Maddison, the population of Western Europe and its main offshoots jumped from 144 million in 1820 to 372 million in 1913.[1] Population in Western Europe kept growing through the twentieth century, accented by a couple of baby booms, but birth rates continued to decline. By the first decade of the twenty-first century, we have Western Europe slowly entering the third stage of demographic transition. The offshoots, particularly the US, are also aging but at a much slower pace due to the benefits of large-scale immigration.

Thus, over a period of two hundred years, the West has gone through a remarkable demographic transformation. However, it is Asia that presents the more dramatic spectacle of demographic transition both in terms of the speed of change as well as the sheer scale of the populations involved. Japan led the way but, one by one, other Asians have followed.

According to UN Population Division statistics,[2] Japan was significantly younger than the US and the UK in 1950. The median age in Japan was 22.3 years, about the same level as India and China. In comparison, the UK and the US had median ages of 34.6 years and 30 years respectively. Demographically speaking, Japan was still a pre-modern society. However, Japan then underwent very rapid demographic change. The median age jumped to 30.4 years by 1975 and by 2005 to 42.9 years. The UK and US aged too but the trajectory was far smoother. The median age in the UK and US in 2005 stood at 38.9 years and 36 years respectively. Japan had gone from being significantly younger to becoming significantly older within half a century. The UN forecasts that by 2025, the average Japanese will be over 50 years old.

The rapid aging of Japan is the first of its kind in Asia but is not unique. The other Asian tigers also went through a similar transition with a lag and China is the latest manifestation of this phenomenon. Indeed, China has experienced a faster rate of demographic change than any of its predecessors because of the 'one child policy'. As recently as 1975, China's median age was 20.6 years, marginally above India's 19.7 years. However, this jumped to 32.5 years by 2005 and is projected to rise to 39.4 years by 2025. In comparison, India has gone through a much slower change. The median age had drifted up only to 23.8 years by 2005 and even in 2025 it will still be a comparatively young 29.9 years.

For our purposes, it is useful to re-interpret this transition in terms of the three demographic phases. In 1975, both China and India were in the first phase with around 56 per cent of the population of working age (defined here as 15–64 years).[3] However, by 2005, the proportion had risen to 71 per cent for China while that for India had drifted up only gradually to 63 per cent. Thus, China rushed into the second demographic phase in the 1980–90s while India has ambled along. According to the UN's population projections, China will remain at its demographic peak between 2005 and 2015, and will rapidly age thereafter.

Meanwhile, birth rates have slowly drifted down in India and the country is only now entering the second phase. Its share of working-age population will rise steadily over the next three decades, overtaking an aging Japan in 2010, and eventually hitting its peak in the mid-2030s. In other words, India will be going through a demographic experience in the next three decades similar to what happened in East Asia in the second half of the twentieth century. This has profound implications for the Indian economy.

Savings and the Asian Miracle

Demographic shifts have a huge impact on economic performance. Most obviously, a changing age structure has a direct impact on the supply of labour and arguably on its ability to absorb new technology (younger workers are more open to new technologies). The UN's projections suggest that India's working age population will rise from 691 million in 2005 to 829 million in 2015 and 942 million in 2025 before stabilizing at around 1050 million in the late 2030s (it will only begin declining in the late forties). By this time, India will have the single largest pool of workers in the world, bypassing an aging China. This means that we have entered a phase where the labour supply will be growing at a very rapid pace for a prolonged period of time. However, the increase in labour supply is not the only impact of demographic change. An equally important impact is that on the supply of capital.

There is evidence that demographics have a strong impact on domestic savings rates as per the Modigliani 'life-cycle hypothesis'. According to this hypothesis, the working population has a much higher propensity to save than the dependent population (young and old). Consequently, when the demographic bulge raises the share of working-age adults in the population, the overall propensity to save rises sharply.[4] Several empirical studies suggest that the impact of this phenomenon in emerging Asia has been dramatic in the last few decades. Williamson and Bloom[5] as well as David, Canning and Graham[6] argue that falling youth-dependency explains the savings boom in East Asia during the 1950–90 period, and that demographic shifts were a key ingredient (perhaps even the most important ingredient) that drove East Asian economies during their 'boom' phase.

The Asian development experience consists of a self-reinforcing growth dynamic fed by the deployment of ever more labour and capital—both driven by the demographic transition process. Increased saving rushes through the banking system and raises the investment rate and this in turn generates employment for the expanding labour force. Employment growth generates incomes that then further boosts savings. This is how China's investment rate has jumped from 20 per cent of GDP to almost 50 per cent over the last three decades. Readers will recall that Japan's investment rate had similarly risen to over 40 per cent of GDP in the early seventies.[7]

Of course, rising domestic savings would not necessarily fund domestic investment in a world of perfect capital mobility. However, cross-border capital mobility is less that perfect and savings tend to bottle up inside the country as long as governments follow reasonable economic policies. This is not a new finding and was first established by Feldstein and Horioka in 1980[8] but subsequent studies have repeatedly confirmed this result. The bottled up savings cause a sharp decrease in the domestic cost of capital and a sharp increase in the quantum of resources available to the financial system (perhaps this explains the charge of financial repression often levelled against these countries). In turn, this results in a lending boom, job creation and consequently even more savings. This process of escalating deployment of labour and capital generates a period of high growth that is often dubbed the 'Asian Miracle'. It has transformed Asia in the last half-century.

India's Savings Boom

The above model of the Asian Miracle depends crucially on a sharp increase in domestic savings feeding an investment boom.

Those who think that China's investment boom is driven by foreign capital should note that its investment rate of around 48 per cent of GDP is less than the savings rate of around 51 per cent of GDP. This means that despite the huge investment effort (including plenty of wastage), the country still has money left over to run a current account surplus and fund the US current account deficit. Today's China needs foreign investment for technology and international business linkages, but not for the money. China essentially absorbs all the foreign inflows into its foreign exchange reserves and thereby lends it back to the world.

India has traditionally had a low savings rate by East Asian standards although it did drift up over the decades. Low savings rates combined with lacklustre foreign inflows meant that capital was scarce. Till 1991, what little capital was available was pre-empted by the public sector or allocated according to administrative diktat. Allocation improved with liberalization but capital was still scarce and expensive in the nineties. This was an important hurdle in the way of investing in mega-infrastructure projects and in large industrial capacity.

If the demographic experience of the rest of Asia is any indication, however, India too should now see a sharp increase in domestic savings. In fact, this is already happening. The country's savings rate was 23 per cent of GDP in 1991 and remained roughly at the same level till 2001. However, it has been rising rapidly in recent years. The latest reading shows that it jumped to over 35 per cent of GDP in 2007. Backed by the pool of domestic capital, the Indian banking system expanded at an unprecedented rate after 2003 (lending growing by over 30 per cent in some years). This is the macroeconomic backbone of the entrepreneurial boom that we encountered in Chapter 3. Moreover, this process promises to escalate. The current population dynamics implies, according to my estimates, a savings rate of over 45 per cent of GDP by 2020. Such a high rate of domestic savings would mean that, even ignoring foreign investment, the scarcity of capital will no longer be a constraint to the economy—a fundamental change in the Indian economic model. We will return to the implications of this later in this chapter, but let us first look at another fundamental shift that we are witnessing at the same time.

The Primary Education Revolution

Whenever I talk about how India's labour force will grow into the future, there is inevitably a pessimist who will retort that it did not matter because illiterate workers are of no use in a modern economy. I agree that illiterate workers cannot be deployed for much more than subsistence agriculture and artisan manufacturing. However, I disagree with the assumption that the average Indian will always remain illiterate. One of the most dramatic sociological changes of recent years has been the spread of primary education across the country. The achievement has gone largely unsung even in India and most public debate still assumes that the bulk of the population is illiterate, and that it will remain so for the foreseeable future. This perception is partly the result of past experience—the very slow spread of literacy in the first fifty years after Independence. With the socialist government focussed on creating the elite public-sector institutes, the literacy rate rose gradually from 18 per cent in 1950-51 to 52 per cent in the mid-nineties. Yet, this area has been revolutionized in the last decade.

Let us first consider the statistics. Between 1990 and 2003, the primary school enrolment rate went up from 80 per cent to almost 100 per cent of the relevant age group. Even socially backward states like Uttar Pradesh, Rajasthan and Madhya Pradesh are now registering gross primary enrolment rates of well over 90 per cent (in some states it's over a hundred per cent because some older students are also enrolling for basic education). The shift is even more dramatic for girls where the proportion has jumped from 64 per cent to 96 per cent during this twelve-year period. It is also significant that 63 per cent of the students stayed on till middle school in 2003 compared barely 42 per cent in 1990. As a result, there has been a palpable drop in illiteracy across the country. Almost half of India's population was illiterate in the mid-nineties but a decade later this proportion had fallen to a third of the population, and is falling rapidly. Indeed, the age structure will ensure that the proportion of illiterates will decline significantly through natural attrition even if no additional efforts were made in improving enrolment. In other words, the pipeline of workers that will hit the job market in the next two decades will be literate. According to my calculations, we can reasonably expect the literacy rate to rise to over 90 per cent by 2020.

Some critics will, of course, question the statistics. However, the difference is palpable from first-hand experience in some of the country's remotest corners. Until fifteen years ago, a traveller visiting a remote rural hamlet could expect to be followed around all day by a band of children demanding sweets. Most of them would not have attended school and freely wandered around the village or helped their parents in the fields. Today, one is likely to witness groups of children— sometimes barefoot and yet in uniform—walking to/from school. Even when a band of children does follow around the visitor (almost exclusively out of school hours), they are more likely to ask for pencils and erasers than sweets. This is not just true of the more developed states but even of inaccessible villages in Arunachal Pradesh, Ladakh, Assam and Rajasthan. I have personally visited good quality schools in areas where there is no electricity, no paved roads and where the morning assembly is routinely disturbed by wild elephants. This is an amazing story that is waiting to be discovered.

This is not to say that more should not be done for primary education, but merely an observation that ground realities are changing very fast. What caused this change? The cumulative impact of years of effort by the government (under the Sarva Shiksha Abhiyan), NGOs, religious charities and dedicated individuals has been an important factor that has engineered this change. A number of innovative schemes were used in many states to encourage enrolment from poor families—for instance, providing free midday meals to students. However, there has always been dissatisfaction with the effectiveness of government schools in the more remote and backward districts of the country. There are numerous instances of truant teachers and schools that exist only on paper. What has really tipped the balance in recent years has been the growth of fee-charging rural schools run by private parties (sometimes in conjunction with NGOs and religious organizations, but often purely as private commercial ventures).

Small numbers of privately run schools have long existed in rural India but their numbers have grown explosively since the late nineties. They are usually quite modest affairs—charging less than Rs 80 per month (about US$2) and have less than a hundred students each. However, they sprung up across rural India on the private initiatives of thousands of small local entrepreneurs (not dissimilar to what we saw in the cable television industry). James Tooley and Pauline Dixon were amongst the first to highlight this phenomenon and their findings have been confirmed by subsequent studies.[9]

What is interesting is that it is the poor who prefer to send their children to these fee-paying schools rather than to free government-run schools. A study by Murlitharan and Kremer[10] shows that private schools are more common in areas that are poorer and where the government-run system was dysfunctional. For instance, half of the villages in the relatively poor states of Uttar Pradesh, Bihar and Rajasthan had private schools, while the relatively well-run state of Gujarat had very few.

Moreover, they found that private-school teachers were on average ten years younger that government school teachers, more likely to have college degrees and usually came from the same village. Private-school teachers were far less likely to be absent even though they were paid a fraction of what government school teachers were paid. Not surprisingly, they also found that private-school students have better attendance and higher test scores. This is why the poor are willing to sacrifice their meagre savings to secure a better education for their children.

Most interesting of all, interviews found these poor parents (often themselves illiterate) demand that their children are taught English from the primary level! Since government schools in many states introduce English only at the secondary level, the poor prefer to pay to opt out. In fact the main constraint is not the willingness of poor parents to pay for better schooling but the supply of English-speaking teachers who can meet this demand.[11]

In my view, the primary-education revolution has very important implications for India's growth trajectory. India has long had a skewed human-capital profile with a highly educated urban middle-class combined with a largely illiterate hinterland. This is an important factor that fed India's unique growth trajectory—the common picture of bullock-carts transporting food to feed some of the world's most talented rocket-scientists and software engineers. However, this disjunction may be about to change. As the impact of the primary education revolution feeds through the age structure, the country will suddenly have a pool of human capital that fills the middle ground. These are not people who can write complex software but can at least follow basic instructions and run simple machinery. In other words, the combination of population dynamics and improved literacy should lead to a sharp increase in the availability of blue-collar workers over the next two decades.

A New Trajectory

The post-liberalization trajectory of the Indian economy was sparing in its use of scarce capital and relied on deploying skilled but inexpensive white-collar workers. Now the circumstances are changing. White-collar workers are becoming more expensive as the services sector boom uses up the middle-class and, thereby, is making wage arbitrage unattractive. At the same time, we have seen how a demographic shift is already driving up the savings rate and making capital easily available (even ignoring inflows of foreign capital). The same demographic shift will also make available a mass of working age workers most of whom, for the first time, will be literate as a result of the primary-education revolution. This means that we are witnessing the emergence of an environment where India's competitive edge will lie in the deployment of capital and bulk labour rather than skilled white-collar workers.

This new circumstance is very similar to what existed in other Asian countries at the time of 'take-off'. Japan entered the second phase of demographic transition in the late fifties. It had a literacy rate of over 90 per cent at that stage. Over the next few decades, other East Asians like Korea, Taiwan and Singapore experience a similar shift in both demographics and in literacy. China entered the second demographic phase in the late eighties with a literacy rate of around 80 per cent. In each case, 'take-off' saw a sudden increase in savings rates and in mass deployment of cheap (and literate) labour. Within a generation, the process created infrastructure, industrial capacities and raised living standards.

Over the next few years, India will see both a sharp increase in literacy rates as well as in the share of working age population. The initial conditions are, therefore, already in place for an East Asian-style 'miracle' driven by heavy investment and low-skill employment—an economic trajectory that is very different from what India has witnessed thus far.

Not everyone is impressed by the Asian growth model. Economist Paul Krugman[12] suggested that such growth is somehow disreputable because it is driven more by bulk deployment of labour and capital rather than through cutting-edge innovation. They feel that immature financial systems misallocate the growing pool of resources and cause the process to break down. The Asian Crisis of 1997 is seen as a vindication of this prognosis. It is true that growth through this route has its risks, especially the possibility of a major misallocation of capital. However, there can be no doubt that it can deliver very rapid growth to an underdeveloped economy and upgrade standards of living at an unprecedented pace. It cannot be denied that the Japanese and the Singaporeans enjoy some of the highest standards of living on the planet today.

Moreover, factor accumulation does not just bulk up past technologies but allows the absorption of new technologies. These may not necessarily be scientific innovations that win Nobel Prizes but they allow for large productivity gains for the host country as new infrastructure is put in place and new technologies are imported. In other words, there is nothing wrong for a developing country to generate growth by using investment and literacy to absorb technologies that already exist in the rest of the world. The more important issue is whether or not these societies remain open to new ideas and influences. The Soviet experiment did not fail because of its emphasis on heavy investment but because of its inability to grasp the messy process of risk-taking and innovation.

In fact, it can be reasonably argued that Europe itself went through a process that parallels the East Asian experience, albeit spread over centuries. There is evidence that literacy rose steadily from the seventeenth century. Britain was one of the first places where it happened. Records show that 64 per cent of men appearing as witnesses in diocesan courts in Gloucester between 1595 and 1640 could at least sign their own names.[13] Although female literacy remained very low, this was still a sharp improvement on earlier centuries. Through the eighteenth century, literacy gradually spread to Britain's North American colonies and eastward across the rest of Europe. This allowed the mass application of new technologies.

Of course, unlike present-day Asia, Europe had to make most of its own innovations—but there was little choice for the first-mover. Even then it is not strictly true that the rise of Europe was totally due to indigenous innovation and not diffusion of knowledge. After all, the European Renaissance would not have been possible without the absorption of foreign ideas such as Indo-Arab mathematics and Chinese printing techniques. Moreover, the Industrial Revolution occurred in Britain rather than on Continental Europe although eighteenth-century Britain had only a small advantage over the rest in cutting-edge science. The real difference was that Britain was more literate and, following the rise of the middle class, more open to new ideas. It was therefore more able to generalize the scientific advances. It was the democratization of innovation and the diffusion of ideas that made Britain great.

Even as literacy spread, Europe went through a demographic shift as death rates and then birth rates declined. The change in population dynamics began in late eighteenth-century France and then spread very gradually through Europe in the nineteenth century.[14] The process continued well into the twentieth century and caused dependency ratios to decline (this is now reversing as Europe ages). In turn, this led to the accumulation of capital and investment. The gradual increase in literacy and investment then allowed the gains from scientific discovery to be absorbed into the economic system. Indeed, Max Weber's 'Protestant Work Ethic'[15] is all about hard work and thriftiness (i.e. deployment of labour and capital). The difference is that Asia went through this shift within a very concentrated time period.

As one can see, the difference with Asia is not the process but the time frame—the process took several centuries in the West and a few decades in Asia. Note, too, that the West experienced all the pains associated with this route including misallocations of resources and major financial crises. The nineteenth and early twentieth centuries are full of such shocks: the panics of 1819, 1837, 1857, 1873, 1884, 1890, 1893, 1896, 1901, 1907 and 1910 (not to forget the Great Depression). Asia has a far better record despite the 1997 crisis and all the banking problems of Japan and China. In other words, India is going down a very well-trodden path to development and prosperity. It may need to be extra careful about the efficiency of its financial system but otherwise should not shy away from taking advantage of this opportunity.

Medium to low technology manufacturing is an obvious area that can benefit from the availability of cheap capital and labour. During the socialist era, India's closed economy manufactured the whole range of industrial products as imports were discouraged. This created a very diversified but inefficient industrial base. As we have seen, liberalization led to large-scale restructuring in the late nineties. This dramatically improved productivity but most of the new growth was concentrated in the high-end of the technology spectrum—automobiles, pharmaceuticals, heavy engineering and so on. Traditional areas such as textiles were not the new stars. This was in keeping with the overall high-skill/low-capital investment trajectory that we saw in the post-liberalization period. Going forward, however, the pendulum should swing the other way. India will now copy China and begin building massive factories employing tens of thousands of workers.

Another area that could witness mass deployment of labour and capital is construction—both that of real estate and of basic infrastructure. The country needs new homes, offices, bridges, roads, and airports. The construction techniques used in the country today are some of the most backward in the world. It is still common for construction workers to build brick by brick, using materials carried on their heads. Most of the roads are still built by wielding pick-axes and pouring boiling tar by hand. The availability of capital and literate labour will change all this in the same way it changed in other parts of the world. It will simply become worthwhile for contractors to use workers who know how to use modern construction equipment. In turn, this will improve the quality of construction and the speed of implementation.

The services sector too could begin to change by boosting segments that use semi-skilled workers. Segments that could be transformed are retailing and the wholesale-supply chain. India's retail sector is currently dominated by small family-run shops. This is a very inefficient system of distribution since it ties up a large section of the newly emerging middle-class (i.e. the increasingly educated children of the local shopkeeper). In contrast, organized large-scale retailing would allow a few white-collar workers to leverage a mass of blue-collar workers to efficiently supply an ever-growing range of goods to a rapidly growing consumer class. Changing tastes and attitudes will multiply the pace of transformation. In other words, the country's future will be more about basic services, mass manufacturing and large construction projects rather than software exports and high technology.

Can Poor Infrastructure Stop India?

Till a few years ago, very few people would have believed that India was capable of sustaining GDP growth of over 6 per cent for any length of time. When I began arguing from the late nineties that India was capable of generating Asian-style growth rates, I was usually met with disbelief and occasionally ridicule. Things have changed since then and many people would now accept that India can potentially sustain growth of 8 per cent or more. However, their optimism is based on the belief that India's middle class can keep driving growth by applying its skills to the high technology services sector. Unfortunately, for reasons already discussed, this cannot be relied on to sustain growth for too much longer.

Fortunately, India is already in the midst of a major shift in population dynamics and in the spread of basic education. History suggests that there is a good chance that India too will take this path and re-enact the Asian Miracle. This implies a massive expansion in bank lending, heavy construction, manufacturing and basic services. However, there is still an engrained view that India cannot recreate its high-technology success in other areas. Some of the arguments are spurious and cannot be taken seriously, including, for instance, the argument that Indians are not 'culturally' disciplined enough to be used in mass manufacturing. However, there is one counter-argument that always comes up and needs to be taken seriously—that India does not have the physical infrastructure to generate Asian-miracle type growth.

It is true that India has very poor physical infrastructure when compared to the rest of Asia. The first thing that strikes any visitor to India is the poor state of the country's airports, roads, power-supply and stock of urban real estate. Clearly, this imposes a large cost on the economy. However, it is not right to assume that growth in manufacturing and construction will become possible only after the infrastructure problems have been resolved. This is a very 'static' perspective of the development process. From a 'dynamic' perspective the current state of affairs presents an opportunity—after all, it is the process of creating infrastructure that generates hyper-growth. To understand this let us look at how people perceived the future prospects of countries like Korea in the fifties.

In the 1956 edition of the Grolier Society's *Lands and Peoples* encyclopedia, Korea's economy is described thus—

'The country is almost entirely agricultural with rice, barley, wheat, beans, and grains the chief crops. Cattle of good quality are raised and whale fishing pursued. Silk-worm raising is carried on. Gold, copper, iron and coal are abundant. The principal exports are rice, beans, peas, pulses, hides, cattle, silk, cocoons and gold; and imports include cotton goods, silk goods, machinery, kerosene oil, grass cloth, sugar and coal. Interior transport is by pack horse, oxen, rail, motor cars and by river. Before the outbreak of the Korean war in 1950, there were 1676 miles of railway in operation. Length of telegraph line 5496 miles and telephone line 5991 miles.'[16]

The India section of the same encyclopedia reads thus:

'Agriculture is the chief occupation. India has more acres (over 50 million) under irrigation than any other. To further increase agricultural output, the government is supporting a number of new large reservoir and irrigation projects. The principal crops include millet, rice, corn, wheat, barley, tea, sugarcane, cotton jute and rubber. Chief industries are weaving of cotton cloth, production of tea, jute, steel and cement, metalworking and silk raising. The most important minerals are coal, petroleum, chromite, iron, mica, magnesite, and manganese. Leading exports: raw jute and cotton, tea, spices, textiles hides. Chief imports: manufactured cotton, metals, machinery and grain.

Railroad mileage, about 35,000, mostly government owned. There are some 90,000 miles of surfaced road. Length of telegraph line is 113,500 miles. Air service is maintained within and beyond India.'

It is clear from these extracts that just fifty years ago it was India that was thought to have better infrastructure and a somewhat more evolved economy. Not only did South Korea have poor infrastructure, it had been devastated by war and partition (in fact, much of above mentioned infrastructure had been lost to the communist North). Yet, it was South Korea and not India that industrialized first. It is not enough to say that Korea was able to rebuild itself just because it was supported by the West. There are many Asian countries that were supported by the West in the fifties and sixties, and did not fare particularly well in subsequent decades—Philippines, South Vietnam, and Pakistan, to name a few.

The critical ingredients in South Korea's favour, in my view, were the radical changes in literacy and demographic conditions. Therefore, when the country's outward-oriented economic policies generated demand for infrastructure, it was able to respond by applying easily available capital and labour to build the infrastructure. Note how this process is self-reinforcing by generating both the demand for materials as well as the means to supply them. Every other successful Asian country started out with poor infrastructure and used the demographic/literacy shift to create it. In other words, poor infrastructure should be considered a constraint only at a point of time. When seen from a dynamic perspective, infrastructure can be created—this does not merely allow new economic activities but its construction, an important economic activity in itself.

This brings us to the question of whether or not the availability of labour and capital is enough to trigger an infrastructure building boom in India. Infrastructure development in many areas has been held up for years due to misplaced and unclear government policy. However, it is also true that there are several areas where Indian infrastructure has dramatically improved. The telecommunications sector is an obvious example of how a sector can go from being a constraint to becoming a strength within a very short period of time when a good policy framework is put in place. We are now witnessing significant improvements in a number of other areas—ports, highways and airports. Even the long-forgotten railway network is enjoying renewed investment and productivity gains.

Admittedly, many improvements have proved to be inadequate to meet subsequent demand, but this merely proves my point about this being a self-reinforcing process. Growth is generated as each shortage triggers a supply response. The problem is never the shortage but the ability and willingness to respond. Given the pipeline of capital and labour, India's poor infrastructure should be less a problem and more an opportunity. Good policy leadership can certainly speed up the process of infrastructure building but it would now take extraordinary effort to stop the process itself.

Can India Generate Enough Jobs?

The first decade after liberalization (i.e. the nineties) was before the demographic shift. The share of working-age population was not rising exponentially. Therefore, a change in school enrolment was good enough to temper expansion in the labour force. The situation is about to change. According to the projections of the UN's Population Division, India's working age population will rise from 691 million in 2005 to 829 million in 2015 and 942 million in 2025 before stabilizing at around 1050 million in the late 2030s. Even if youth participation rates were to continue to decline because of growth in secondary and tertiary education, there would still be a very rapid expansion in the labour force. Besides, employment generation by industry and services will have to accommodate a large-scale shift away from agriculture (which still employs full-time or part-time some 55 per cent of the workforce).

This is where the Asian model really kicks in. The growth that we have seen thus far is a 'bonus'—a reward for shifting from an inane set of policies to more sensible ones. But now, the real game is about to begin. As the pool of domestic savings rises to around 40–45 per cent of GDP, capital will flood through the financial system. All of a sudden capital will become available for projects on a scale not seen before in the country. Manufacturing companies will begin to create facilities that employ tens of thousands of new workers—not dissimilar to what we see today in China. Similarly, the retailing sector will need to employ workers in the thousands to man their outlets and procurement networks in order to supply the boom in consumption. At the same time, construction companies will have to employ ever more workers to create new townships, bridges, highways and power-stations. Note how most of these jobs are not for the educated middle-class but for those with basic education. High-skill workers will now be too valuable to be used as the engines of growth and will now be deployed to manage and direct the process.

The above scenario is not a far-off dream but is already happening. After years of restructuring, Indian manufacturing companies were in very trim shape by the turn of the century. They were some of the most profitable and efficient companies in the world, and were operating in a market that was growing at break-neck speed. Most of them initially resisted the temptation to expand capacity and hire more workers because of the painful memories of the late nineties. However, they could not hold back for long. Opportunities were expanding so fast that more and more manufacturers began to hire workers from 2003. At the same time, given the spirit of the time, many younger workers have opted to become self-employed entrepreneurs and have further generated new jobs. The trickle has become a flood.

The OECD Employment Report for 2007 estimates that India generated 11.3 million jobs between 2000 and 2005. This is the highest expansion anywhere in the world. Even China managed only 7 million during the period and all of the OECD countries together managed only 3.7 million. While the data cannot strictly be compared across countries, it does underline the fact that India does not suffer from 'jobless growth' as alleged by some critics of liberalization. Employment growth averaged 2.8 per cent per annum between 2000 and 2005 which kept up with labour force growth and was higher than population growth.

As this book was being written, large investments were being planned in virtually every sector. In a thought-provoking article in November 2006, *Business Standard* editor T.N. Ninan wrote about how the statistics from a survey of 550 companies showed that job creation was not only growing but growing exponentially.[17] Large corporates like Reliance and the Tata Group were announcing mega-projects in the retail sector. In November 2006, Bharati announced a tie-up with Walmart; three days later the Aditya Birla Group announced its plans to enter the field. Meanwhile, construction companies like DLF and Unitech were announcing their intention to build whole new townships across the country. This does not merely create jobs for construction workers but also thousands of permanent jobs for electricians, carpenters, shop-assistants, security guards, taxi-drivers and others that are needed to make these new townships and facilities function.

A year later, as the draft for this book was being finalized in November 2007, the newspapers were full of how there were serious shortages of even blue-collar workers. DLF announced plans that it would try to bring back 20,000 Indian construction workers from the Gulf region.[18] The Minister of State for the Railways, R. Velu, told a press conference that the Railway system had 162,000 vacancies. An impatient Reliance decided that it needed to import 4,000 Chinese construction workers to lay gas pipelines. Employment is no longer a problem for India, if there is a problem it is employability. However, for the blue-segment at least, help is on the way in the form of demographic bulge and the literacy shift.

In other words, the bulk deployment of labour has already begun and is not just a trickle-down from the middle-class boom. As it grows, it is creating a momentum of its own. The newly employed blue-collar workers will shop from the new discount stores, buy motorcycles, visit the movie theatres and eventually aspire to their own apartments. Within a generation, some of these families will use education and entrepreneurship to move into the middle class. All this happened in East Asia during their demographic shift. The phenomenon has been clearly visible in major Indian cities like Mumbai, Bangalore and Delhi for a few years, and now we are about to see it spread to the smaller towns across the country. Watch out for the Nagpurs, Allahabads and Jodhpurs—and then for the Purulias and Jhansis.

The necessary initial conditions for the spread of the growth dynamic are falling in place but they may not be sufficient to trigger the virtuous cycle growth, savings and investment. There are many countries that have gone through the demographic shift without being able to take advantage of it. Civil-war ravaged Sri Lanka is an example of a country that went through the transition but was unable to capitalize on it. It is also not certain that the virtuous cycle, once triggered, would be smoothly sustained over the entire second demographic phase. The Asian Crisis of 1997 demonstrated how the virtuous cycle can by violently disrupted by a poorly functioning financial system. It took many years for South-east Asian countries to recover from the Crisis. Given these caveats, the demographics and literacy revolutions should be seen as creating an opportunity that needs to be actualized through 'second-generation reforms'.

The problem for policy-makers is that there is a danger of being overwhelmed by the sheer number of changes that are needed in a country of India's size. So it is important to focus the reform effort on those areas that are likely to have the highest payback. This book is not the place to list the vast number of necessary policy changes and then prioritize and sequence them. However, I will now take the liberty to discuss on a single area that I feel is critical—'general governance'. More specifically, I will focus on the need for reform in the legal system. The legal system provides the key institutional framework that is necessary for the millions of social and economic interactions that make a market-based economy work. As any Indian will understand, a good game of cricket needs more than just good players—it needs rules and reliable umpires.

7

The Importance of
Institutional Reform[1]

Governance and Second-generation Reforms

The cumulative impact of fifteen years of liberalization has transformed India. However, the process of liberalization has been slow, erratic and patchy. Policy makers were not just held back by political considerations but were constrained by the sheer scale of changes that were needed and by the considerations of sequencing. Therefore, outdated and inefficient practices still pervade the economic system and myriad areas remain where reforms are still sorely needed. The need for more change is widely recognized and we regularly hear demands for 'second-generation reforms'. So, what are these second-generation reforms and how are they different from the first-generation ones?

The first generation of reforms was about liberalizing the

economy from the constraints of an inward-looking, public sector-dominated arrangement. At this stage 'liberalization' and 'reform' meant the same thing. Therefore, the first fifteen years of reform were about de-licensing the industrial sector, opening the country to foreign trade and investment and so on. Many commentators now argue that the next generation of reforms should follow up with changes such as full-fledged privatization and changes in labour laws. We have seen how the tertiary-education system needs to be opened up. However, strictly speaking, privatization, university reforms and labour laws are unfinished business from the first generation as they are still largely about liberalization.

Second-generation reforms are a fundamentally different set of changes. They are about adjusting existing institutional arrangements in order to support the new 'market-based' economic system that has emerged as a result of liberalization. In essence, this is about building a healthy new relationship between the State and civil society in general and the economic system in particular. The first generation of reforms was about reducing the role of State so that the private sector could expand. This has been achieved to a large extent despite various remaining anomalies. The next generation of reform is about reforming the State itself and helping it play its rightful role in the new India. There are a wide array of necessary changes ranging from administrative reform to improvements in the provision of public goods and services.

Perhaps the most important service that the State fills is the provision of general governance. The term 'general governance' is difficult to define formally although most people would agree on what it means. I suppose, one can say that general governance is the systemic order that needs to be maintained so that people can engage in economic and social interaction. Virtually all economic and social ventures require collaboration that would not be possible without 'trust' that each party would carry out their end of the bargain. In turn, this trust is based on the rules of engagement and their enforcement. From the very beginning, therefore, economists have recognized the role of the State in creating and enforcing these rules. One need do no more than read Kautiya's *Arthashastra* or Adam Smith's *Lectures on Jurisprudence* (1762–63) to realize how much emphasis even the earliest economists placed on the State's role in ensuring general governance.[2]

The Role of the Legal System

The legal infrastructure is the key institutional framework through which the State provides general governance. In the context of post-liberalization India, the legal infrastructure plays a number of important roles. First, it is the means through which the State can create a generalized environment of trust so that various economic entities can interact with each other. This is always true to some extent, but it is even more true in a market-based economic system where resources are no longer being allocated according to the government's administrative diktat. The mass deployment of large amounts of capital and hundreds of millions of workers needs clear rules of economic engagement and the even-handed enforcement of large numbers of contracts. The legal infrastructure is the key institutional framework that ensures this. Most importantly, it is the one institution that is necessary to ensure that the benefits of growth trickle down. After all, it is the poor and the weak who most need help to ensure that their rights are protected in the market-place.

Peruvian economist Hernando de Soto has long argued that the success of capitalism in some countries and its failure in others has much to do with the systemic ability to define and enforce contracts (particularly in the case of property rights). Of course, the State is not necessarily the only institution that can provide rules of engagement and ensure enforcement. There can be a number of other sources of 'trust' ranging from religion to social/family linkages. Avinash Dixit and Francis Fukuyama have extensively discussed such alternative arrangements.[3] In a vast and socially diverse country like India, however, it is probably not wise to rely on such informal systems as the primary source of trust. At best these systems can compliment the formal system and at worst they can be harmful. For instance, in the state of Bihar, the lack of State provision of governance has led to the creation of caste-based organizations/networks that have further undermined generalized trust. Thus, we need to be mindful of the possibility that 'Bad forms of Governance' can drive out 'Good Governance'. A robust legal system is the best insurance against this.

Second, the legal system is important because it is the means through which Justice is administered. It is important to recognize that Justice is a good thing in itself, over and above the impact it may have in encouraging systemic trust. Economists are usually utilitarian at heart and tend to ignore this, but others would probably consider the provision of Justice as a distinct and commendable service in its own right. The provision of Justice must be a central part of the redefined, post-liberalization State and, therefore, legal reform must be a focus of second-generation reforms.

Third, the legal infrastructure can itself be an agent of change in common-law countries like India. This is a role that is most often ignored by economists because the legal system is seen as the blind and passive enforcement of a static body of rules. This may be largely true of those countries that function in the civil-law judicial tradition where the judiciary is merely expected to interpret a given legal code and no more. However, in the English common-law tradition, each judgment creates a precedent that can be used in future cases. In other words, each judgment effectively creates a new law. This is a major advantage of the common law system as it allows an endogenous system of updating laws without having to revert to legislative intervention for every small change.

The Indian judicial system belongs firmly to the English common-law tradition (except in a few areas). This is potentially an important strength for a country that is undergoing rapid change. In a civil-law system it would be almost impossible for the government and the legislature to constantly update and coordinate a huge body of laws and sub-laws. Indeed, it may be easier to create a completely new body of law as China has been attempting to do since 1978.[4] However, even this does not solve the problem because in a rapidly developing country the new laws themselves may become outdated very quickly and need to be replaced. The effort of coordinating these changes through the mass of laws and by-laws is great, especially if the changes are constantly subject to democratic scrutiny. In contrast, India can potentially use its judicial system to percolate reforms through the economic system. Once a general principal has been established by policy-makers or the legislature, other rules can be changed on an ongoing basis as and when disputes are brought to the courts. In other words, a good judicial system can be an active agent of change in India rather than just a passive enforcer.

Given these above factors, the legal system can play a very central role in post-liberalization India. As we will now discuss, the Indian legal/judicial system has fallen short of all the three objectives. It is not surprising, therefore, that eminent thinkers like Bimal Jalan and Arun Shourie have repeatedly pointed to this as an area of failure.[5] This is unfortunate because the underlying judicial institutions are good and the system should have been a very major strength for the country. Therefore, legal reform must be a focus area for second-generation reforms.

The Rules

Broadly speaking, the legal infrastructure is made up of two elements. The first element is the body of laws and regulations. These are the rules of engagement. The second element consists of the arrangement that enforces the laws—the police, the judicial courts, tribunals and so on. In addition, there are the legions of 'inspectors' employed by different government departments to ensure compliance with various regulations. Regulatory bodies like the Reserve Bank and the Securities Exchange Board of India may also be considered a part of the enforcement mechanism, although they have very specialized jurisdictions. It would be tedious to try and encompass all forms of enforcement in this chapter. For the purposes of discussion, therefore, we will restrict ourselves mostly to the mainstream judiciary although we must keep in mind the wider context.

India has a very large body of laws and regulations. Given the federal constitutional arrangement, there are national-level laws as well as state-level laws. In addition there are local government laws as well as administrative laws—these last include a plethora of rules, regulations, orders and administrative instructions issued by various government ministries and departments.

The first problem with this body of law is that no one seems to know what all these rules are or even how many exist. The number of Central Statutes is often estimated at between 3,500 and 2,500 although there are estimates that are at a totally different level of magnitude.[6] In short, we are not even sure how many Central statutes are in existence. It is even more uncertain how many state-level laws are in effect. The Jain Commission had estimated that in 1998 there were between 25,000 and 30,000 state-level statutes in existence in various parts of the country.[7] Note that this estimate was an extrapolation of laws existing in a single state and can hardly be considered a very good statistical sample. Matters deteriorate rapidly from here as there is not even an estimate of administrative and local laws. The Jain Commission had been set up to review administrative laws but could not even get a full set of rules, regulations and administrative instructions issues by the Central government. The number of administrative laws at the state, district or municipal level is simply unknown.

The second problem with the existing body of law is that a large number of them are now very old and often dysfunctional. Many of these laws were enacted in the nineteenth century and, in theory, remain in effect. Here are a few of the Central statutes that are still in effect: Bengal Indigo Contracts Act 1836, Bengal Bonded Warehouse Association Act 1838, Shore Nuisances (Bombay and Kolaba) Act 1853, Bengal Ghatwali Lands Act 1859, State-Carriages Act 1861, Sarais Act 1867, Oudh Talukdars Relief Act 1870, Chhota Nagpur Encumbered Estates Act 1875, Bikrama Singh's Estates Act 1883, Mirzapur Stone Mahal Act 1886, Lepers Act 1898. This is merely a small sample of old Central statutes. The number of outdated state laws and administrative regulations number in tens of thousands. For instance, the regulations under the Factories Act 1948 still stipulate that factories need to be whitewashed (other paints will not do), drinking water must be provided in earthen pots (water coolers will not do) and sand must be provided in red-painted buckets (fire extinguishers will not do).[8]

Some readers may think that these old laws are harmless but we have repeatedly seen how these laws are invoked in cases that have no relationship with their original context. For example, the Sarais Act of 1867 makes it a punishable offence for inn-keepers to refuse drinking water to passers-by. This was used by the municipal corporation a few years ago to take a Delhi five-star hotel to court. Similarly, the Indian Telegraph Act of 1885 has been invoked many times by state-owned broadcaster Doordarshan over telecast rights for cricket matches. This nearly derailed the telecast of the Cricket World Cup of 1996. As one can see, there is ample scope for using these outdated rules for harassment, bribery and rent-seeking. Of course, many other countries have old laws. In a functioning common-law system these old laws should not be a problem as the judiciary could update them by creating a precedent whenever a case comes up, but this requires a robust and quick judicial process.[9] This is not the case in India and this is a topic that we will return to later.

The third problem with the body of law is that there is little internal harmony or consistency. Many laws contradict each other. Definitions and classifications are not standardized. Some areas are absurdly over-regulated while others do not have meaningful laws. Labour laws provide a good illustration of how confusing the legal framework can be for an employer. According to the Indian Constitution, this is an area on the Concurrent List—meaning that there are both national-level laws and state-level laws. It appears that there are almost fifty laws just at the national-level together with associated rules and regulations. These include not only general laws such as the Industrial Disputes Act 1947 and the Factories Act 1948 but also a number of specialized laws. For example, there are at least three Acts related to just to the beedi[10] industry: the Beedi and Cigars Workers (Conditions of Employment) Act

1966, Beedi Workers Welfare Cess Act 1976 and the Beedi Workers Welfare Fund Act 1976.

In addition to these fifty-odd Central labour laws, there are a plethora of state-level laws and administrative directives that also apply. On top of these labour laws, there are several other state and Central laws that indirectly affect labour such as the Dangerous Machines (Regulations) Act 1983. What makes it worse is that many of these laws are inconsistent and often contradict each other. Note that I am not commenting here on the content and quality of these laws. That is a large area of debate in its own right. I am merely pointing out the sheer complexity of the legal framework related to the simple, routine act of employing workers.

Not surprisingly, such a confusing body of law makes it difficult for everyone to understand the rules of engagement. Even if a person was diligently law-abiding, it would be virtually impossible for that person to function without knowingly or unknowingly breaking some rule. Indeed, much of the booming call-centre outsourcing business is technically illegal according to some state laws. In 2005, the Labour Ministry of the Haryana Government invoked Section 30 of the Punjab Shops and Commercial Establishments Act 1958 to disallow women from working night shifts at call centres and outsourcing units in the town of Gurgaon. Women typically account for 40 per cent of the workforce and the very nature of outsourcing requires them to work night shifts since they are servicing clients in Western countries. Clearly, the ban would severely affect the business model of this sector. The matter was still under dispute at the time of writing but it highlights the dangers of having a body of law that is complex, outdated and sometimes blatantly absurd.

Enforcing the Rules

While there are many problems with the legal rules for social and economic engagement, the enforcement of the rules is an even bigger problem in India. Enforcement is dependent on a number on agencies and institutions including the police, the judiciary, inspectors from various government departments and so on. Nonetheless, the judiciary can be said to be the critical lynchpin of the formal enforcement mechanism because it is the main arrangement for dispute resolution. The Indian judiciary is a large and complex world consisting of the Supreme Court, the eighteen High Courts and the Subordinate Courts (which number in the thousands and include district-level courts, magistrate courts, fast-track courts and so on). In addition, there are a number of other quasi-judicial bodies including special tribunals and pre-trial dispute resolution forums like the Lok Adalats.

Most observers would agree that the biggest shortcoming of the Indian judicial system is the very slow pace at which cases are processed. Even routine cases sometimes get bogged down for decades in the judicial quagmire. As a result, the system has a large and growing backlog of cases. According to a recent Law Ministry estimate that was widely quoted in the press,[11] there were over 25 million cases pending the court system at the end of 2005. These include 32,000 in the Supreme Court, 3.5 million in the High Courts and 22 million in the subordinate courts. This does not include the large number of cases stuck in various tribunals and quasi-judicial bodies. Note that over 80 per cent of the cases pending in the High Courts are civil cases while criminal cases account for only 12–15 per cent. The situation is totally different in the subordinate courts where two-thirds are criminal cases. Thus, the reader will appreciate why the Indian judicial system is seen as such a drag on general governance.

Although there is no objective measure to prove or disprove this, it is generally agreed that the Indian judiciary (at least the higher echelons) has a good record when it actually does pronounce a judgment. Of course, there may be occasional miscarriages of justice but it is accepted that mistakes are unavoidable in any large system. However, I think such a prognosis is too lenient—justice delayed is justice denied even if the eventual judgment is the correct one. This point is best illustrated by the infamous Uttam Nakate case.[12]

In August 1983, Nakate was found at 11.40 a.m. sleeping soundly on an iron plate in the factory in Pune where he worked. He had committed three previous misdemeanours but had been let off lightly. This time his employer, Bharat Forge began disciplinary proceedings against him, and after five months of hearings, he was found guilty and sacked. But Nakate went to a labour court and pleaded that he was a victim of an unfair trade practice. The court agreed and forced the factory to take him back and pay him 50 per cent of his lost wages. Both parties appealed against this judgment (Natake wanted more money). The case dragged on through the judicial system for another decade and in 1995 another court awarded Nakate more money because he was now too old to be rehired. Bharat Forge eventually had to approach the Supreme Court and in May 2005—more than two decades after the original incident—the apex court finally awarded the employer the right to fire a worker who had been repeatedly caught sleeping on the job.

The above case is usually taken as an illustration of the country's ridiculous labour laws. However, it is an equally good illustration of the miscarriage of justice by the judicial system. The first generation of reforms did not made a dent on labour laws; they are largely the same today as they were in the early eighties. The Supreme Court's final judgment was based on the interpretation of laws that have not changed. The judicial system could have arrived at this common-sense result at any stage of the proceedings (after all, the facts of the case were not really in dispute, Nakate always accepted the fact that he was sleeping). Therefore, one should not be impressed by the fact that that the judicial system eventually got the judgment right.

The failure to deliver justice is even more pressing in the criminal-justice system. As already mentioned, two-thirds of the pending cases in lower courts relate to criminal cases. This reflects two forms of gross injustice. First, there are a very large number of undertrials who are left in limbo, many of them forced to live in jail as they cannot afford bail or do not have the legal support to apply for it. Indeed, an estimate shows that in 1996, 72 per cent of all prisoners in Indian jails were undertrials. Many of these prisoners had been in jail for years without coming to trial and some may have long exceeded the maximum sentences for their alleged crimes.

There is no peace for even those let out on bail. They are repeatedly summoned to the court but their cases are not resolved. The recent case of Abdul Gaffar is a shocking illustration of the state of affairs. Abdul was a sherbet seller in Mumbai and was arrested in May 1993 on charges of breaking in and stealing two cans of oil in December 1992. He was charged for trespass and robbery. For the next fifteen years, the poor sherbet-seller was summoned to appear in court almost every two weeks but his case was never heard. Finally a special court heard him in March 2008 and the case was dismissed within an hour.[13]

Meanwhile, the judicial system seems unable to identify and punish genuine offenders. According to Bibek Debroy, the conviction rate is less than 5 per cent! The Jessica Lall case is a well-known example of this problem. Jessica Lall was an upcoming model. On 29 April 1999 she was working as a celebrity barmaid at *Tamarind Court*, a bar-cum-restaurant frequented by socialites. At 2 a.m., a group of young men led by Manu Sharma entered the bar and demanded a round of drinks. Jessica Lall refused since the bar was already closed. Manu Sharma, so the story goes, lost his temper and shot her dead. This incident was witnessed by several people and they reported it immediately to the police. After a manhunt that lasted several days, Manu Sharma was arrested.

The case was brought to trial in August of that year and almost immediately began to run into trouble. One by one the witnesses turned hostile and changed their story. What would appear at first sight to be an open-and-shut case dragged on for years. Eventually in February 2006, Additional Sessions Judge Bhayana freed Manu Sharma and his friends. Indeed, he agreed with the defence counsel that the 'police had decided to frame the accused'. It is believed by many that Manu Sharma was able to use his political connections (his father is a powerful politician belonging to the Congress party) to subvert the judicial process. There was a public uproar and the Delhi High Court has now allowed an appeal against the judgment. Under pressure from public opinion and intense media scrutiny, a re-trial finally convicted Manu Sharma in December 2006. His lawyers are now in the process of appealing to the Supreme Court.

We are not concerned here with whether or not Manu Sharma is guilty. The above case is merely an illustration of how the legal system is unable to enforce some basic laws in even the national capital. Of course, this is not just the fault of the judiciary since it also involves other agencies such as the police (in this case, the witness protection mechanism has been a particular failure). However, this distinction between various arms of the State is not relevant from our perspective. The point is that the enforcement of laws is a serious concern. It also does not matter to the economy at large whether the miscarriages of justice is in commercial or criminal cases because both of them are a part of overall general governance. This is why I strongly feel that the post-liberalization State must make this its central focus.

The Importance of Legal Reform

Given all the issues discussed above, it should be no surprise that one should wish for reforms in the legal system. The broad legal infrastructure is necessary for providing both a formal set of rules for social/economic interaction as well as a means for enforcement. However, this is even more relevant in post-liberalization India where we expect a market-based economic arrangement to bring prosperity to the country, particularly to the poorest sections of society. As pointed out by economists like Hernando de Soto, market-based systems work to reduce poverty only when there is an integrated formal system of enforcing contracts (especially in the case of property rights). According to Hernando de Soto, this is the key reason why market-based economic systems are so successful in some countries but fail in others.[14] Failure on this front is both unjust to the weaker sections of society but also risks unnecessary social conflict.

This point is especially pertinent in today's India when we are witnessing large land-transactions to build new cities, industrial units and 'Special Economic Zones'. This land is being acquired largely from small farmers, often using an 'eminent domain' argument. Not surprisingly this is leading to many conflicts over fair compensation and property rights. In 2007, we saw how these arguments can turn violent. The state government of West Bengal had proposed to acquire a large tract of land in Nandigram for setting up an industrial unit.

The local population vociferously objected. On 14 March 2007 a group of 3,000 policemen were sent in to force the acquisition. There are allegations that they were joined by armed members of the ruling Communist Party of India (Marxist).

The villagers had anticipated this and barricaded themselves—roadblocks were set up and crude homemade weapons were stockpiled. What happened next is highly controversial but by most accounts the police opened fire and several villagers were killed (the numbers range from 11 to 50).[15] The matter then spiralled out into major political storm. There were more violent incidents and more casualties. Ultimately, Chief Minister Buddhadeb Bhattacharya was forced to publicly apologize to the people.

Given the large number of proposed 'Special Economic Zones' and new construction projects, these conflicts will become very frequent in the near future unless there is a quick system of resolution that is trusted by all parties. Unfortunately, we have seen how the Indian legal infrastructure is currently unable to cope with this requirement. The poor farmers of Nandigram did not feel that they could get justice by approaching the courts and therefore felt compelled to rebel. In fact, there are large tracts of central India where the institutional failure to protect the rights of the poor has inflamed Maoist rebellions. This is a major failure and second-generation reforms should try to redress it as soon as possible.

Finally, a good legal system can be an important partner in furthering the reform process itself. It is virtually impossible for the executive and legislative arms of the State to keep up with all the rules governing a vast and rapidly changing country like India. Even if all existing possibilities are taken into account by formal legislation, there will always be unforeseen circumstances that will emerge. Thus, what is needed is a system that endogenously renews itself. India's common-law based judicial system can potentially fill this role but it must be made capable of doing this quickly and consistently.

There are many things that need to be done in order to improve the Indian legal infrastructure. The body of law should be rationalized through both legislative and administrative initiatives. Many outdated laws should be scrapped or replaced. Similarly, efforts should be made to simplify legal provisions in areas with a multiplicity of rules and regulations. The process of enforcement and dispute resolution also needs radical changes. These include changing court procedures, introducing modern technologies in the judicial process (including full computerization of records), improving training and management in the lower courts, and harmonizing basic definitions. There is also need to increase the number of judges. At present, India has 13 judges per million population compared to 107 for the United States, 73 for Canada and 51 for Britain. This is not just a matter of creating new positions but of filling up existing vacancies. There are currently thousands of vacant judicial posts. There is also a need alter the system of Appeals—the current system encourages everyone to appeal to higher courts against the decisions of lower courts. This is major reason why cases drag on for so long. Finally, the government itself should re-look at this own role as a litigant. At present, a very large proportion of cases involve the government (often on both sides).

This is not the place to discuss the various necessary reforms in detail. Much has been written about it over the years. Law Commissions are periodically instituted to suggest necessary changes and the interested reader may read through their various reports. The main purpose of this chapter is to draw attention to the central importance of legal reform within the context of second-generation reforms. Unfortunately, this area is usually seen as peripheral to the economic reform process and only rarely attracts attention in the wider debate. In my view, however, this is probably the single most important area requiring reorganization and it would have dramatic multiplier effects through the rest of the economy. The role played by the Reserve Bank and SEBI as regulators in improving the functioning of the financial system in the last ten years illustrates how a good set of rules and their even-handed enforcement can dramatically improve performance.

What makes it even more attractive is that it is unlikely to require a great deal of additional public expenditure. No formal estimates are available of how much money would be needed to set the judicial system right but my guesstimate is that to stabilize the judicial backlog at current levels (together with significant quality improvements) would need an additional allocation 0.12 per cent of GDP worth of fixed investment and around 0.06 per cent worth of annual recurring costs. Even if it actually costs a multiple of this amount, it is a very small amount of money compared to likely systemic gains. Besides, it would probably pay for itself through increases in court fees and general tax collections.

This is all very well, the reader may say, these problems are well known. Why should things change in the future? Luckily, there is reason to be optimistic because Indian society and political economy are being fundamentally transformed by the myriad forces we have so far discussed in this book. Let us take a peek at this future.

8

How India Will Change

The second half of the twentieth century was a truly remarkable period in Asian economic history. After falling behind the West for four centuries, one by one Asian countries have closed the gap to a greater or lesser extent. Japan led the path. It was followed by what were once called the Newly Industrialized Countries of South Korea, Taiwan, Hong Kong and Singapore. Till the Asian Crisis cut the process short, countries in South-east Asia too appeared to be following this well-trodden path. China is merely the latest manifestation of this process. In each case the sequence of events has been almost exactly the same—a sharp improvement in literacy, a demographic shift and an outward-oriented policy regime have caused an investment-driven growth boom. We have also seen how the Asian growth model shares many of the basic elements of the process that drove growth in Europe during its 'take-off' years.

India is just entering the hyper-growth phase. Here is the prospect of sustaining high GDP growth rates over decades and of eliminating extreme poverty and want. Here is an opportunity to reverse a thousand years of civilizational decline. The process is likely to transform India dramatically over the next few decades. The changes will be felt at all levels— through urbanization, evolving socio-cultural values and growing international influence.

Inevitable Urbanization

An important implication of the new growth paradigm is urbanization. Historical experience shows that economic development has almost always led to the growth of cities. The West experienced this first and, for instance, 80 per cent of the population of the US today lives in urban areas. The proportion is even higher in some of the other developed countries. Just as East Asia's pace of development has been exceptionally fast over the last half century, its pace of urbanization has also been exceptionally rapid. As always, Japan was the first to go through the process and one by one other Asian countries followed. Even in relatively underdeveloped Indonesia, urban centres now account for 48 per cent of the population.

Yet again, China is the most recent and most dramatic example of the phenomenon. Since the early eighties, China's rate of urbanization has matched its explosive GDP growth rates. The share of urban population in China was only 12 per cent in 1951 and had drifted up very gradually to 18 per cent by 1978. However, rapid industrialization dramatically quickened the pace in the last twenty years, and the proportion is said to now be around 55 per cent. If anything, this is an underestimate of the scale of urbanization because Chinese cities have large populations of unregistered rural migrants who live and work there without official permits. The country has responded by pouring concrete—almost overnight it has built up new highways, housing estates, airports, malls, office blocks and so on. It is said that with the urbanization of China, more than half of the world's population now resides in cities for the first time in history.

Urbanization is the sociological and spatial counterpart to economic processes that shift workers away from subsistence agriculture to more productive sectors. It is the physical manifestation of all the construction activity that accompanies rapid growth. In other words, it is an integral part of the growth process. However, rapid urbanization would be a major break from India's past as the country has been, so far, a reluctant urbanizer. It took half a century for the share of urban population to rise from 17 per cent in 1951 to 28.5 per cent in 2001. Indeed, the overwhelming majority (i.e. more than 70 per cent) of Indians still live in villages. This marks India as one of the last major rural societies in the world.

The slow pace of urbanization is not the only oddity of Indian urbanization. Whatever urbanization has happened over the last few decades has been concentrated in the larger cities. The broader metropolitan areas of cities like Delhi, Mumbai, Bangalore and Hyderabad have grown at an exponential rate while the small mofussil towns across the country have stagnated. As a result, almost 40 per cent of the country's urban population lives in cities with populations of more than a million. Those living in cities with more than 10 million people account for 15 per cent of the urban population (the agglomeration around Mumbai alone is said to have 19 million). The comparable ratio for China is 5 per cent.[1]

What is the reason for this pattern? One could argue that the urbanization experience thus far is probably a reflection of the pattern of overall development since Independence. The slow pace of generalized industrialization (which would have fed the smaller towns) combined with a booming educated middle-class (which is concentrated in the large cities). As these mega-cities have grown, they have attracted migrants both from rural areas and from the smaller towns in order to feed the top–down growth pyramid. In turn, this has led to the many slums that dot all Indian cities. This schematic explanation is attractive but it is mere conjecture. In truth, there are virtually no studies that have tried to understand India's urbanization process. There are several studies of the urban poor, the socio-economics of Mumbai's slums and even of the state of urban infrastructure. However, none of them have a comprehensive model of what is driving or inhibiting urbanization in the country.

This general apathy towards understanding India's cities is possibly a reflection of a widespread notion that India is fundamentally a rural nation, and that it will always remain so. Many influential leaders including Mahatma Gandhi had held an idealized view of Indian village life and this may have influenced official and academic interest in the subject.[2] Urbanization, therefore, is seen as an anomaly that is taking the country away from its 'true' identity—a problem that should not be encouraged or investigated.

This is particularly unfortunate because India was the centre of the earliest urbanized civilization in the world. The archaeological remains of the Indus Valley civilization bear testimony to the fact that five thousand years ago Indians lived in well-planned cities. Dozens of sites scattered across north-western India and what is now Pakistan show standardized city plans with streets laid out in grids, complex sewage systems and public baths. Even the bricks were of a standardized shape and size. Their quality was so good that millions of these ancient bricks were unknowingly used to lay railtracks in the late nineteenth and early twentieth centuries (until the archaeologists Sir John Marshall and Dayaram Sahni decided to investigate where all these bricks were coming from).

Given the experience of the rest of the world, the urbanization of India is all but inevitable. The questions are—what form will it take, and is the country prepared for this? The World Urbanization Prospects (2007 Revision), published by the UN, projects that 197 million Indians will move to urban areas between 2007 and 2025, but I think this level could be hit much faster if the economy is consistently able to sustain GDP growth rates of over 8 per cent. In my view, India's population will be 40 per cent urbanized by 2025, and that it will be an urban-majority country by around 2040.

In other words, Indian cities need to prepare for the influx of hundreds of millions of people. In 2007, the urban agglomerations around Mumbai and Delhi contained populations of 19 million and 15.9 million respectively. The UN's projections suggest that by 2025, Mumbai will have 26.4 million people and Delhi will have 22.5 million. In other words, these cities will be the second- and third-largest cities in the world (Tokyo will remain the largest with 36.4 million).[3]

Although the above statistics suggest enormous expansion for the mega-cities, they will actually lag behind overall urban growth. The logic of India's new economic trajectory will mean that this growth will come increasingly from the smaller cities, long-forgotten mofussil towns and, most interesting of all, the building of brand new urban centres. In turn, this will spur demand for economic and social infrastructure including transportation links, schools, hospitals, office blocks, temples and so on. This will be the story of India for the next three decades.

The problem is that such a massive scale of urbanization requires vision and serious municipal planning. Unfortunately, the demand for urban real estate will grow so fast that existing institutional structures may well be left far behind. Large townships are already being built but with little thought to public transport networks and waste disposal. Take, for example, Gurgaon—a flashy boom-town, south of Delhi, that has emerged almost overnight with shopping malls, condominiums and swank office towers. It is often touted as a 'planned' development. Yet, it does not even have a municipal waste-disposal system. Garbage and raw sewage is simply taken some distance away and dumped. Similarly, no thought was given to public transport till very recently. As a result the city, still half-built, already suffers from serious traffic jams. Virtually no provision has been made for social amenities like museums, temples, theatres and so on. The developers have not even bothered to put in pavements for the brave few who may wish to walk.

A very similar story can be told of the once beautiful city of Bangalore. The lakes and gardens that had originally attracted the talented to the city have given way to malls, housing estates and corporate towers. Of course, rapid growth is inevitably chaotic to some degree but, as a frequent visitor to both cities, one cannot help thinking that it could have been managed better. It defies belief that in an era of high oil prices, India is still building new cities based exclusively on privately owned automobiles (especially careless when India itself has no oil). As an afterthought, metro-rail systems are being built for Bangalore and Gurgaon but they have already been developed in a way that is unfriendly to public transport. I do not doubt that the country has the resources and expertise to build the necessary infrastructure but India has still not woken up to the inevitability and scale of the phenomenon. It is time that the inevitability of large-scale urbanization is recognized and a capable institutional structure is created to deal with it.

Beautiful it may not be but urbanization will change the way we think of India as an economy and as a society. As more and more people move to cities all over the country, the dominant culture of India will become 'urban'. By this I mean that traditional links to the 'native village', extended family and caste will weaken; old ideas will erode and new attitudes will emerge; consumer tastes and aspirations will change.

The most interesting impact of urbanization will be the continued growth of the urban middle class. As it grows in size, it will make ever more political demands—for better institutions of governance, for better education and for better urban amenities. It is the growing political and economic clout of this group that will play a critical role in shaping India's destiny.

The Middle Class and Institutional Change

In a study of economic development over very long periods, Charles Jones found that sustained development was always accompanied by improvements in institutions that promoted innovation and risk-taking—most importantly through the enforcement of contracts and property rights. 'The most important factor in the transition to modern growth has been the increase in the fraction of output paid to compensate investors for the fruits of their labour.' In other words, for India to take advantage of the emerging opportunities, it needs an institutional infrastructure that encourages hard work, innovation, risk-taking and the pursuit of excellence.[4]

We have already seen how the legal infrastructure is not really up to the task, but it is a specific example of a more generalized problem. At the macro-level, we find that corruption and inefficiency remain rife through the bureaucracy and the political system. The main thing that has changed in the first fifteen years of liberalization is that an open economy has reduced the scope for rent-seeking in many areas. At a more local level, the lack of local government institutions continue to create municipal squalor that is unacceptable even for a country in India's level of development. In my travels around the world, I have visited many countries that are just as poor or even poorer than India but I have rarely encountered the squalor that one associates with Indian towns.

The British had left behind some good institutions when they left India in 1947—courts, a body of law, municipal systems, a civil service and so on. These were far from perfect but they did provide a basic framework that was far ahead of the rest of the developing world, especially what existed in most of East Asia. Unfortunately, these institutions were left to decay after Independence and in many cases were deliberately subverted to serve political ends. As a result, India today lacks the institutional structure that is needed to take full advantage of the opportunities that are coming its way.

India is hardly the first country to have faced the institutional constraint to development. So what are the factors that have allowed these institutions to develop in some countries and not in others? To understand this we need to go back to the Industrial Revolution in late eighteenth-century Britain. It was not just the first country to industrialize but was also the first to develop the institutions that encouraged the organized risk-taking and innovation that characterize industrial capitalism.[5] The reason Britain developed the market-friendly institutions was that they were demanded by a new and powerful group that emerged by the eighteenth century—the middle class.

The key characteristic of the middle class is its value system—the belief that one can change one's station in life through hard work and education. The elite still exists but they are not fossilized as in the pre-modern value system where hereditary aristocratic privilege defined one's station in life. The occasional individual may have broken through the arrangement but it was rare. Thus, when the middle class becomes more politically powerful it demands institutions that allow social fluidity. As Surjit Bhalla puts it, 'So economic freedom, in all its manifestations, is the first demand of the middle class.'[6]

The emergence of the British middle-class as a political force began a lot before the Industrial Revolution of the late eighteenth-century. In the previous century, the kingdom had been witness to a series of events that had seriously weakened the monarchy and the old feudal power-structures. The English Civil War (1642–51) between the Royalists and the Parliamentarians ended with victory for the latter. King Charles I was tried and executed, and Charles II was exiled. For a while the country was a republic headed by Oliver Cromwell. Although the monarchy was later restored, real power would remain in the hands of the Parliament. This was further consolidated when James II was ousted by the Parliament and replaced by William of Orange following the Revolution of 1688. As a result of these political changes, gradually power shifted to a wider spectrum of society including the small but emerging mercantile middle-class. Britain would therefore be the first major country where economic relations were defined by contractual obligations rather than aristocratic rent-seeking. When the British colonized North America, they took these attitudes with them.[7]

On the continent, the Dutch were the first to develop a powerful middle-class but with the French Revolution the transfer of power to this group spread across Europe. The old aristocratic arrangement was violently overthrown. It is telling that Napoleon Bonaparte, a middle-class Corsican, would rise to rule over much of Europe. The combined forces of Europe's royalty would eventually defeat Napoleon but old Europe had been thrown open.

As the middle class grew in strength it increasingly demanded more changes. In Britain, it culminated in the Great Reform Act of 1832. Prior to this reform, the Parliament was dominated by the landed nobility who used their influence to get themselves and their nominees elected. The more senior members of the nobility could influence multiple constituencies. The Duke of Norfolk, for instance, is said to have 'owned' eleven constituencies. The middle class found this especially unfair because the booming new industrial cities were given little representation while many sparsely populated rural areas were over-represented. The Great Reform Act changed all this by increasing the franchise dramatically and by giving representation to the new industrial centres. In doing this, it gave effective political power to the middle class who used it to further strengthen market institutions.

The middle-class outlook was transmitted very early to North America by British settlers. From the very beginning, the settlers in North America placed a great deal of emphasis on higher learning—Harvard College was set up in 1636. By the time the United States became independent, the middle class was a powerful driver both in Britain and in its former North American colony. Note the contrast with South America which bore the brunt of a feudal Spanish conquest. There land-ownership rather than education was prized, and a middle class grew far more slowly. As a result, the institutions of governance have remained stunted in most places even today.

Now contrast all this with the situation in eighteenth-century India. Many scholars have wondered why India or China were not the countries to have had initiated the Industrial Revolution. India, for instance, had the world's leading cotton-textile industry till the early eighteenth century, unbeatable for quality, variety and cost. For centuries, the industry had not only satisfied domestic demand but had also supplied textiles for export throughout the Indian Ocean, particularly to Southeast Asia. With the arrival of the European traders, there was a boom in demand for Indian-made textiles. Why did the Indians not invest in new technology to expand production to meet this demand?

The explanation put forward by well-known scholars like David Landes is that this was because India had a huge abundance of cheap labour and there was no incentive to invest in machinery. Instead, Indian merchants simply deployed more and more workers to work the same technology. This is a very unsatisfactory explanation because this incentive structure changed after the Industrial Revolution once Britain clearly demonstrated the superiority of production techniques that used machines. Surely Indian merchants of the late eighteenth and early nineteenth century could see that mass deployment of labour was no longer competitive without the new machinery. Why did they not change?

India's failure to industrialize is the result of two factors. First, eighteenth-century India did not have the human capital capable of developing or internalizing the 'modern' production techniques. From the eleventh century, the 'closed' cultural milieu did not encourage the sort of scientific innovations that were being made in Europe. Moreover, an almost entirely illiterate industrial workforce was unable to make the myriad small adjustments necessary to work and upgrade to the new production chain.

The second factor was that the institutional environment in India was simply not conducive to capital accumulation and investment. The Mughal empire was based on feudal institutional structures that already looked outdated to visiting Europeans in the late seventeenth century. As Francois Bernier, the French traveller, records in his *Travels in the Mogul Empire 1656-1668*:[8]

'Nor can the commerce of a country so governed be conducted with the activity and success that we witness in Europe; few are the men who will voluntarily endure labour and anxiety, and incur danger, for another person's benefit—for a governor who may appropriate to his own use the profit of any speculation. In cases, indeed, where the merchant is protected by a military man of rank, he may be induced to embark in commercial enterprises; but still he must be the slave of his patron, who will exact whatever terms he pleases as the price of his protection.'

In other words, the mercantile class was not strong enough to stand up to the warlords that ruled the country. The only large Indian-run 'factories' of this period were the royal karkhanas but they showed all the enterprise and innovation that one can expect from a feudal-run public sector. At best, the occasional enlightened prince would support a particular project but it was never generalized into an institutional arrangement.

If the circumstances do not look conducive to large-scale fixed investment in the late seventeenth century, matters deteriorated significantly into the eighteenth century. As the Mughal empire crumbled, it was racked by revolt and rebellion. Groups like the Marathas, the Sikhs and the Jats set up their own independent kingdoms while Mughal governors in the Deccan and in Bengal became virtually independent. At the same time the country was under external attack from all sides; the Persians under Nadir Shah and the Afghans under Ahmed Shah Abdali sacked Delhi. The French and the English fought for control over the south.

With so much uncertainty, merchants must have felt that

the institutional framework was not predictable enough to allow large-scale investment in the new industrial machinery being developed in Europe. In fact, things were so unstable by the middle of the century that the rich merchants of Bengal actually bribed Robert Clive of the East India Company to militarily oust Nawab Siraj-ud-Daulah, thereby initiating the British conquest of India. In short, the lack of stable institutions and governance was a big factor that stopped India from industrializing. Lacking a sizeable middle class, there was no group strong enough to demand these changes. A similar argument can be made for China.[9]

Once British rule was well entrenched, the colonial power did introduce a number of basic institutions—a body of law, a judicial system, a civil service and so on. These changes allowed the emergence of industrial hubs around Bombay and Calcutta. Much of this industrial capacity was British-owned but by the beginning of the twentieth century there were several Indian industrialists. Unfortunately, these institutions steadily fell into decay after Independence and on some occasions were deliberate subverted. Why?

A small middle class did emerge in colonial India. As it developed a political consciousness, it demanded change and freedom. However, in the context of the times, this meant political freedom from British rule. This is why most of the leadership of the Freedom Movement were drawn from this middle class. As pointed out by authors like Pavan Varma, the middle class was very politically active during this period.[10]

However, matters changed after Independence. The upper echelons of the middle class took over the reins of power from the British and overnight became the new aristocracy. The Gandhi–Nehru clan is the most obvious example of this phenomenon. This change in status meant that its attitude towards market institutions changed. The remaining middle class was tiny, perhaps no more than a couple of million individuals. Thus, it was in no position to be able to defend market-friendly institutions against the socialism of the newly elevated elite. Moreover, in the early years, the middle class stood to gain from the new arrangement as it subsidized higher education and created white-collar jobs by concentrating the country's resources in large public-sector projects.

As we have seen, the middle class grew steadily in the decades after Independence but, over time, the inefficiencies of the socialist regime began to tell. Job opportunities dwindled and the middle class grew more restive. Those who like sociological explanations for history may think that it was pressure from the middle classes that eventually led to the reforms of 1991.[11] It is true that the middle class has played an important role in many important historical turning points in world history. However, in this particular case, the middle class was not the decisive factor. Despite all its problems, the middle class in the late eighties still had a stake in the faltering public sector. Liberalization promised new but uncertain jobs but it threatened the end of a way of life.

More importantly, however, the middle class was not politically powerful enough to demand change. First, it was just too small. There is no good estimate of the middle class in 1991 but we have seen that even in 2007 it was just 50 million. Furthermore, the section of the middle class that had emerged from the housing colonies was far more pan-Indian and less rooted in their provinces. This happened at a time that the gradual spread of political awareness was making the poorer sections increasingly active. This meant that when the middle class was becoming more pan-national, the country's politics was becoming more local—witness the steady growth of powerful regional and caste-based parties like the Rashtriya Janata Dal and the Bahujan Samaj Party. The middle class found that it was too small to count on its own steam and too rootless to be able to influence increasingly localized politics.

As a result, the urban middle-class largely lost interest in politics. The new urban middle-class has so far remained less politically active than either the old elites or the poorer masses. Even today, the old nobility and descendants of the pre-Independence middle-class (and later elite) provide a far larger share of the political leadership than the rootless middle class that emerged from the public sector and the housing colonies. Virtually every one of the 'young' leaders that entered the Lok Sabha (Lower House) over the last decade came from powerful political families. At the other end of the spectrum, there are many political leaders who have emerged in recent years from relatively modest backgrounds. In contrast, the urban middle-class has thrown up very little. How different this is from the earlier generation of politically active middle-class Indians described by authors like Pavan Varma. This is why it was an external crisis rather than pressure from the middle class that led to the reforms of 1991.

Fortunately, this situation will not last forever as the Indian middle-class is growing. As the country shifts to the Asian Miracle growth paradigm, the middle-class will no longer be the 'source' of growth but its 'result'. As more and more blue-collar workers are deployed in the booming economy, many of them will work their way up the social ladder. McKinsey Global Institute projections suggest that the middle class will grow from the current level of 50 million to 583 million by 2025. Strengthened by the growing numbers, the middle-class will begin to demand its share of political power. In turn, it will demand the institutions of governance. A study by William Easterly shows that sustained development of institutions in various countries is critically influenced by what he calls the 'middle-class consensus'. As with many long-term changes, it is a dynamic that feeds itself—more growth will generate more middle class and this will support growth-enhancing institutional changes.

This will be a radical shift in the country's political dynamics and the first signs are already visible. In recent years, the middle class has been increasingly successful in using the mass media to weigh against blatant misuse of political power. In both the Jessica Lall murder case and the similar Priyadarshani Mattoo murder case, the middle class used the mass media to indict the politically powerful. The phenomenon is now widening. In 2005, under sustained pressure from social activists, the Lok Sabha (Lower House) enacted the Right to Information Act which gives the general public access to government records. Transparency is good for all sections of society but it is a potent weapon in the hands of the middle class.

As the middle class grows more numerous, it will be able to influence politics more directly. Middle-class politicians will emerge to represent middle-class electorates. As happened in Britain with the Great Reform Act of 1832, the middle-class will demand the delimitation of constituencies to reflect the growth of the new urban centres and changing population concentrations. The delimitation process has already begun and the regular recasting of constituencies will eventually change the balance of power. According to the proposals of the Delimitation Commission of India, Mumbai city will see the number of Lok Sabha (Lower House) representatives drop from three to two while the number of constituencies in the suburbs will rise from three to four. One could think of this as a shift from the old middle-class of South Mumbai to the new middle-class that lives in Ghatkopar and Andheri. As India urbanizes, there will be shift from rural areas to the new urban centres.

In other Asian countries, the rise of the middle class led to profound changes in socio-political power structures. South Korea was ruled by a series of military dictators till the mid-eighties. There were several attempts to establish democracy but they did not take root. However, as the economy grew, the middle class grew in strength and eventually was strong enough to demand change on its own steam. In 1987, the middle class led a series of protests against the government of General Chun over the murder of students. These protests eventually forced direct elections and democracy.[12] Similarly, it was political pressure from the middle class that guided Indonesia to democracy after the political and economic crisis of 1997-98 pulled down the Suharto government.

India is already a democracy of long standing but its institutions are in dire need of reform. A rising middle-class will demand necessary changes in the institutions of higher education, and in the institutions of general governance—including the judicial system. In doing this, India will follow the experience of other countries. Thus, there is reason to be optimistic that India too will develop the institutions necessary for sustaining growth.

Westernization Versus Modernization

The growth of the middle class and urbanization brings us to an important friction within India's re-emerging civilization—the tussle between 'Modernization' and 'Westernization'. This has been a key issue from the nineteenth century, particularly due to the importance of English as the catalyst that gave birth to the middle class. The conflict is best illustrated by Ram Mohan Roy himself. It is said that he had two homes—one where he lived with his family and one where he entertained his European friends. His contemporaries used to say that in the first house there was nothing European except Ram Mohan and in the other house there was nothing Indian except Ram Mohan. His successors too struggled with this conflict and each came to terms with it in their own way.

Mahatma Gandhi, for instance, actively rejected Western dress and lifestyle. When asked what he thought about Western civilization, he facetiously replied 'I think it would be a good idea'.[13] In contrast, Jawaharlal Nehru imbibed a great deal of Western culture and was self-conscious about it. He is said to have once joked that he was the last Englishman to rule India. However, like many of his contemporaries, he was in awe of the West and its achievements. Even as he was attempting to modernize India through State-directed investment, he could not bring himself to believe that Indians could compete in the wider world.

However, as India re-emerges as a civilization in the twenty-first century, the new urban middle-class will be less apologetic about its Indianness and far more confident in its interaction with the outside world. This is an important difference with the pre-Independence middle class. Those who were entering the workforce from the nineties were more than a generation removed from British colonial rule. Whereas the earlier middle-class had prided itself on it ability to speak 'propah' English and quote Shakespeare, the new middle-class is both more casual and confident of both its English—and its Indianness. For this generation, a combination of Indian-English and Hindi has already become the common tongue and English is thought of as an Indian language that was accidentally invented in Britain.

This attitude would have pleased Rajagopalachari. At the time of Independence, he had been the most articulate advocate for retaining English. The language, he argued, 'is ours. We need not send it back to Britain with the Englishman.' He added that according to Hindu tradition, all languages were the gift of the goddess Saraswati. Therefore, English 'belonged to us by origin, the originator being Saraswati, and also by acquisition.'[14] Every great civilization borrowed from its predecessors—the Romans borrowed from the Greeks, Islam borrowed from pre-existing cultures in Persia and the Levant, and the European Renaissance was made possible by a rediscovery of its ancient past. In adopting English, this generation of Indians is merely doing the same.

What about the future of indigenous languages? Like the Prakrits, they will thrive as long as they continue to evolve and change. Hindi, for instance, is now understood by almost all Indians below the age of forty. This is not the official Hindi of textbooks. The spread of Hindi has been due to cinema, television and popular music. Thus, the Hindi used outside the heartlands owes more to the Punjabi-laced tongue of Delhi and rough-and-ready street language of Mumbai. Just as English is the language of business and higher education, Hindi is the language of popular culture.[15] India has long been comfortable with the use of multiple languages and will confidently continue to do so in the future.

The new cultural confidence has been reinforced by the growing success of the middle-class diaspora. Some of the top companies in the world are now headed by Indian-born CEOs—Vodafone, Pepsico, Citibank to name a few. How different from the under-confident and lonely individuals described by Jhumpa Lahiri in *The Namesake* and *The Interpreter of Maladies*. It is difficult, therefore, for expatriate Indians of my generation to comprehend the isolation that was felt by Lahiri's characters as they built their lives in a foreign land and an alien culture.

Indians in general and the middle class in particular are becoming ever-increasingly open to ideas and innovations.

However, they are absorbing these influences on their own terms and giving them a uniquely Indian flavour. At the same time, Indian ideas and tastes are beginning to influence the rest of the world. This is Modernization and not Westernization. The attitude can be best summed up as 'We are like that only'.

Modernity, of course, has its own demands. As the middle class grows and urbanizes, the standard family unit is becoming the nuclear family rather than the old joint family. Divorce is becoming commonplace even in the smaller towns. More and more old people are left to fend for themselves without the support of a multi-generational family. The old arranged marriage system is facing stress as the old social networks are dissolving.

This does not mean that Indian society cannot evolve to cope with these new problems. In each case, Indian society is creating unique solutions. Take for example the arranged marriage system. Once it relied on word-of-mouth. Today it is using matchmaking websites like shaadi.com (which claims to be the world's largest matrimonial service). Similarly, the narrow caste-/provincial-based preferences are slowly dissolving in favour of wider choices based on other criteria. A recent survey by jeevansathi.com, another matrimonial website, found that a growing section of the mostly middle-class respondents were looking for partners on the basis of their professions.[16] As the country urbanizes and the middle-class grows, this process will widen.

Still, the process retains a very Indian flavour. Prospective partners are still vetted by the family and enormous efforts will be expended on establishing his/her 'background'. A wedding is still seen as a coming together of families rather than as contract between individuals. Indeed, some cultural traits are being reinforced by the new environment. Big weddings, for instance, are making a comeback after the relative restraint of the socialist years.

The Environment Cost

While growth and development are worthy goals for a poor country, it should be recognized that it comes with its costs. The process of hyper-growth though the mass mobilization of labour and capital is a messy business. It necessarily implies enormous disruptions and dislocations in the human and natural landscape as new cities and factories are built, large populations are relocated, and natural resources are tapped at an accelerated pace. Other societies too faced these problems during their take-off phase. The soot and grime of the industrial cities of Britain during the Industrial Revolution have been immortalized by Victorian literature. Since then, this problem has affected virtually every country that has industrialized rapidly.

As always, China is the latest and most extreme example of this phenomenon. It is estimated that 99 per cent of China's urban population breathes air that the European Union would consider unsafe.[17] According to EU standards, concentrations of dust, soot and aerosols are unsafe at over 40 micrograms. In 2006, Beijing averaged 141 micrograms and it is not even the most polluted place in China. The People's Republic is already the world's largest producer of sulphur dioxide and will soon replace the US as the world's largest producer of greenhouse gases. These are only the statistics related to air quality. There are similarly worrying data for other forms of pollution ranging from water to soil.

India is now embarking on the same journey and there are many signs that the ecological system is already under severe strain. Take for example, the fate of the once-common vultures and sparrows. Since the early nineties, 95 per cent of the Indian vulture population has been wiped out. It turns out that the culprit is a common drug called Diclofenac that is used commonly as a painkiller for farm animals. A vulture that has eaten the flesh of a dead farm-animal treated with Diclofenac dies within 48 hours. The vultures are now near extinction. A similar fate has befallen the sparrows. These were the most common birds of my childhood; so common that we never gave them much thought—they built nests in our homes, flitted around the garden and occasionally stole food. No one quite knows for sure why the sparrows are disappearing but it is a very sad development.

There are many indigenous species that are under threat. A few like the tiger make headlines. However, the sudden disappearance of common species that lived in close proximity of human populations suggests that a fundamental reassessment is required very soon. This is not a sentimental appeal. These species are like the proverbial canary in the mine. The stress that they are feeling is a reflection of underlying instabilities—the pollution in the rivers and lakes, the chemicals that are entering the food-chain, and the worsening quality of air.

The costs of this damage can be very large and they need to be correctly accounted. A few years ago, the Chinese government decided to calculate 'Green GDP'—i.e. national income adjusted for pollution and environmental damage. The preliminary results were sobering. The study found that environmental cost accounted for at least 3 per cent of annual GDP in 2004.[18] In my view, these are very conservative estimates. I have been part of an effort to do the same for India, and the early results are quite worrying.[19] For instance, water quality in the rivers of Uttar Pradesh is now so bad that it would cost 17.5 per cent of the state's GDP to restore it to 'safe' levels.[20]

Rapid economic development cannot avoid some environmental damage, but a little sensitivity and foresight can significantly mitigate the worst consequences of growth. For instance, large green-field cities are being designed in India on the basis of the internal combustion engine. It is inexcusable that, in the twenty-first century, we are recreating American urban sprawl when that model of urbanization has been outdated for years. Gurgaon and Bangalore are textbook examples of how not to build new cities. In both cases, a little bit of foresight and imagination would have dramatically reduced the environmental costs as well as enhanced the quality of life.

Looking ahead, India needs to think seriously about the how to manage the growing amounts of industrial and consumer waste, the dwindling and increasingly polluted water resources and the last remaining forests. If not, it will unnecessarily impose long-term costs on future generations. As a latecomer to the development game, India has the advantage that it can leapfrog various technologies. However, it has one major disadvantage—India may have to go through its development phase at a time that the earth's carrying capacity is at its limit. As Jared Diamond points out in his popular book *How Societies Choose to Fail or Succeed*, many societies through history have committed ecological suicide.[21] Indeed, if some theories of the decline of the Indus Valley Civilization are to be believed, it will not be the first time in Indian history. Thus, together with general governance, environmental management must be an important area of focus for the State in the post-liberalization world. Unfortunately, it is today either ignored or treated as an impediment.

India's Future Place in the World Economy

In 2007, India became a trillion-dollar economy. Adjusted for Purchasing Power Parity, its share of world GDP had risen to around 6 per cent, up from just 3 per cent in 1991.[22] This is still small compared to the economies of China (14 per cent) and United States (21 per cent) but the economy is now large enough to begin affecting the rest of the world in terms of its participation in international trade and finance, as well as its demands on global resources. More importantly, the country appears capable of sustaining very high GDP growth rates by re-enacting the Asian miracle. It is not unreasonable, therefore, to expect that India's role in the world will grow over the next few decades. This is a truly remarkable turnaround for a country that was close to default just fifteen years earlier.

This is no mean achievement in light of the secular decline it suffered over the centuries. The rising importance of India in the world economy is now more than visible—the Western press obsessively discusses the loss of white-collar jobs to India, international investors pour billions into the stock-market, and expatriate Indians plan their return home. But what does the rise of India really mean for the world economy and the international trading network? Who gains and who loses? Will India challenge China as the economic power in the twenty-first century?

India has so far taken a unique growth trajectory and this services-led path has meant that the country does not really compete with China. The conventional wisdom today is that this will remain the case into the future. A recent World Bank study, 'Dancing With Giants', concludes that India's rise will not be 'disruptive' of the world trade system and that its manufacturing sector is not really capable of taking on China.[23] A number of other studies have also come to similar conclusions. However, this is merely a case of extrapolating current trends into the future without taking into account the fundamental processes that drive growth in the Asian growth model.

It is very likely that India will have to shift down the technology chain as its mix of available resources changes—scarcity of skilled white-collar workers on one hand combined

188 **THE INDIAN RENAISSANCE**

with an abundance of capital and low-skill labour on the other. As India shifts to the Asian model, it will begin to compete directly with China. This will happen at a time that many of the factors that drove China will begin to erode. The country's per capita income is rising and wages along the eastern coast have risen quite a long way in recent years. It is true that there are still a lot of poor people in China's interiors but they are also less accessible (and will remain so even after the completion of major infrastructure projects).

More important, China's demographic boom years will not last forever. In fact, the 'one-child policy' has meant that China is aging at the fastest pace witnessed by any country in history. According to the UN's projections, China's population will begin to age very rapidly by 2020. This will not just affect the availability of young workers but will cause a sharp fall in savings rates and, thereby, will make it increasingly difficult for the country to finance massive infrastructure projects and capacity expansions in manufacturing. All this will happen just as India is hitting its own demographic peak, and will put the country in a position to eat into China's exports markets.

The above scenario is not a wild conjecture but a well-established path. The Asian miracle growth model has already caused the growth baton to be passed from Japan to Korea/ Taiwan and then to China. The same dynamics will cause the shift to the next generation of 'miracle' economies like India and Vietnam. The point is that the demographic dividend is time-bound for all countries including China (and, for that matter, also for India). This will create the opportunity for India to cannibalize Chinese manufacturing in the same way China has recently eaten into other Asian countries.

Fantasy? It's already happening. In January 2008, Tata Motors unveiled the 'Nano'—the cheapest car in the world at just US$2,500 per unit. Not even the Chinese had dared to cut costs this far. The event may have fundamentally changed the automobile industry for ever. Already, it has triggered a global scramble to produce cars at prices not imagined before. As time passes, we can expect India to do the same to a range of other products. The integration of India into the world is going to be just as disruptive and exciting as that of China and all its predecessors.

Nonetheless, there is one major difference between the rise of India and other cases. India will be approaching the miracle years after having already enjoyed the middle-class-driven services boom. In other words, India will have an existing high-technology sector that will be far more sophisticated than what existed in most other countries at the time of take off. In this sense, therefore, India will be moving down the value chain as it re-enacts the Asian model. It will do this just as other Asians (particularly China) will be attempting to climb the value chain. As this process evolves, India's economy will end up competing in a very wide cross section of sectors and countries. This means that the competition for markets and resources will become particularly intense and complicated.

Imagine a world where an Indian manufacturing company headquartered in Singapore uses Chinese design inputs to compete against a Korean company that uses Vietnam as its main production hub. This is a world of intra-industry trade, cross-country alliances and complex regional production networks. Such a system already exists in East Asia today and China's integration provides a glimpse of how things may work out. However, in the earlier cases it was a more linear process—each new entrant joined at the bottom of the value chain and pushed their way up. In India's case it will probably be more a case of lateral entry. India will be competing with Japan in some areas while simultaneously competing with China and Vietnam in others.

As India's economy expands and globalizes, we should also expect Indian companies to expand their operations abroad. Past generations of Indians associated multinational companies with foreign domination—partly the result of socialist rhetoric and partly the memory of the East India Company. Future generations, however, will think of Indian multinationals. We are already witnessing the beginnings of this phenomenon. In recent years, more and more Indian companies have acquired foreign operations and companies. As I completed the final draft of this book, Tata Motors acquired Land Rover and Jaguar from Ford.

Of course, this does not mean that national borders will no longer matter. Borders and nationality will remain important in those areas where government policy and international diplomacy have a role—especially in sectors connected with natural resources and energy. Like China, India is not a resource-rich country and, as a late entrant, it will find that many of the existing sources of resource supply are already spoken for or perhaps even exhausted. Therefore, India will be forced to use its growing clout in order to elbow its way in. I do not mean that this necessarily implies some sort of military threat or intervention. China's increasing diplomatic and economic involvement in Africa probably provides a good indication of what we could expect from India. However, this does imply a competitive race that India will have no choice but to participate in.

Hard Versus Soft Power

The rise of economic powers and, more broadly, of civilizations is not surprisingly associated with growing international power. Often, this international stature is backed by hard military power. Since the Industrial Revolution, we have seen how each rising economic power also saw growth in military might—Britain, France, Germany, United States and Japan. In most of these examples, this military might led to colonization of lesser countries and on two occasions to World Wars.

So, does the rise of India imply an aggressive and acquisitive bully? Given the above examples, it is easy to argue that the rise of an economic power is necessarily linked to exercise of hard power because of the very logic of the phenomenon—the need to ensure supplies of raw materials, secure markets and maintain particular kinds of international institutional/political structures.

In view of this historical record, some pessimists may argue that it is inevitable that the rise of new powers like India and China will lead to similar results. Perhaps this will be so but there is an alternative possibility suggested by India's ancient past. India was the world's leading economic superpower for much of recorded history. Yet, with very few exceptions, it never exercised hard power outside of the subcontinent. Instead, India's influence in the world was in the form of 'soft power'—trade, culture and philosophy. From Buddhist temples in Japan to *Ramayana* performances in Java, evidence of this 'soft power' is visible even a thousand years after India went into decline. Moreover, the influence of ancient India is not just limited to old cultural traditions. Whenever anyone in the world switches on a computer, he/she is effectively using a binary logic that would not have been possible without another ancient Indian contribution—the concept of 'zero'.

So what will Indian 'soft power' of the future look like? One example is already visible—Bollywood! India's film industry is already the world's largest in terms of the number of films produced and second largest after Hollywood in terms of its global reach. Indian films and music have long been popular from Morocco to Indonesia. Expatriate Indians have spread them wherever they have settled—the United Kingdom, Singapore, Dubai, and the United States. Despite political differences and government bans, Indian films are watched in every town and village in Pakistan. One of the first things that Afghans did after NATO forces drove out the Taliban was to bring out their hidden collections of Hindi music.

Indeed, war-torn Afghanistan is a good example of Indian 'soft power'. At 8.30 every evening the streets of Afghan cities empty as everyone stays glued to Indian soap operas. The most popular is the family drama *Saas Bhi Kabhi Bahu Thi*. The serial is so popular that the sales of small generators have risen sharply as fans try to beat frequent power blackouts. Less wealthy fans have resorted to using car batteries to power their television sets. Some thieves have even taken advantage of this obsession. When the tyres of a car were stolen in Mazar-i-Sharif during a broadcast, one of the thieves scrawled 'Thanks, Tulsi' on the side of the car (Tulsi is the main protagonist in *Saas*).[24]

The future looks even brighter for the Indian entertainment industry. In recent years, the industry has drastically upgraded itself. The songs and dances are still there, but gone are the flimsy cardboard sets and outdated special effects. The production quality is not far short of Hollywood and Indian producers are increasingly more willing to experiment with new ideas. Of course, the renaissance has not been restricted to cinema. We are witnessing a boom in music and in the visual arts. Half-forgotten folk arts are being revived across India. As quality has improved, Indian art is rapidly becoming more mainstream—London night clubs now routinely play Indian music and Bollywood is steadily widening its appeal outside of the Indian expatriate community in the West. Well-known Indian painters now command global prices at auctions in London and New York even as the re-designed products of traditional artisans sell in fashionable boutiques.

What is most important to note is that the success of Bollywood is a living example of the success of cultural openness. India's entertainment industry is not the product of a purely Indian cultural process but is the mongrel offspring of a wide array of influences, both internal and external. Over the years, Bollywood has copied, twisted and even 'stolen' ideas from other countries and cultures. Indian film crews scour the world to hunt for locations. Indian musicians and directors are entering and exploring the world of Western entertainment. Yet, this has diminished neither the growing global popularity of Indian entertainment nor its unique flavour. Hopefully, the resurgent India of the future will be like Bollywood.

Indeed, that future may already be here and manifesting itself in the unlikeliest of places—the world of sport. India is not known to be a sporting nation and has little impact on world sport since the invention of chess centuries ago. However, in 2008, India organized the IPL Cricket Tournament in which it popularized a completely new version of the game. The matches were drastically shortened (to twenty overs), American-style cheerleaders were introduced, foreign players were allowed in for a domestic tournament and, most interestingly, player fees were hiked to rival those of European soccer players. The game of cricket has been thrown open and India's soft power is responsible.

9

Is India's Rise Inevitable?

Although this book highlights the economic aspect of India's reawakening, it is important that we keep in mind that an economic renaissance is always part of a wider civilizational revival. The very attitudes that encourage economic innovation and risk taking are also those that allow cultural innovation and risk taking. This is why a sustained rise of any civilization is based on the pursuit of excellence at all levels of human endeavour. The European Rennaisance in the fifteenth and sixteenth centuries is an excellent illustration of this phenomenon.

Europe entered the 'Dark Ages' after the decline of the Roman Empire. The great library of Alexandria was burned to the ground and the ancient pagan centres of learning were shut down. Then, for almost a thousand years, Europe went into relative decline. However, the 1400s and 1500s saw a remarkable opening of the European mind. The process began in northern Italy and then spread north and west. Within a relatively short period, we see a succession of brilliant minds, including artists like Michelangelo, scientists like Galileo and writers like Shakespeare.

Today, the Renaissance is remembered mainly for its cultural achievements but this was merely one side of the phenomenon. It is no coincidence that the epoch began in the merchant republics of Venice and Florence rather than in the larger and more powerful kingdoms of Europe. Both of them were first and foremost successful financial centres. Their innovations ranged from the standardized use of double-entry accounting to the trading of financial securities. Remembered today for their patronage of the arts, the Medicis were a family of bankers! In other words, the Renaissance was much bigger than paintings and sculpture. It was an age that produced individuals like Leonardo daVinci with his remarkable curiosity in virtually all fields of knowledge.

Of course, many of these individuals made their contributions despite threats from the establishment. Galileo, for instance, was actively persecuted by the Inquisition. Yet, the European world view had changed enough to allow the questioning of fundamental beliefs. During the Dark Ages, such intellectual innovation would not have been possible. As the spirit of innovation and risk-taking spread across Europe, Western civilization saw a rebirth in all spheres. The process was helped by yet another Renaissance innovation—printing. The technology probably originated in China but it was in fifteenth-century Germany that it was perfected.

The movable type was perfected by two Mainz goldsmiths Johann Gutenberg and Johann Fust. The Gutenberg Bible, the first printed book, was published in 1455. From here the technology spread like wildfire. Within five years we had the first printed dictionary, the *Catholicon*. By 1500, less than fifty years after the first printed book, we had printing firms in sixty German cities and Venice alone had 150 presses.[1] Books were once the preserve of the Church and the very rich, but were now available to virtually everyone. Before printing, the very largest libraries had around 600 books and the total number in Europe is estimated at around a hundred thousand. By 1500, the total has been calculated at nine million. This is democratization of knowledge on a colossal scale.

The person who epitomized this new spirit was Christopher Columbus. Said to be an Italian from Genoa, he managed to convince the Spanish Crown to support a voyage across the Atlantic in 1492. From what we know, he was not an especially talented sailor or navigator. He was not the first to realize that the world was spherical. He totally miscalculated the circumference of the earth and the westward distance to India. He was not even able to comprehend the true scale of his own discoveries. But, he was open to a one good idea—that the world was round—and he had the courage to follow it. In other words, he was not a born genius but a man who was driven by the spirit of his times. This spirit entered many others. Within a few years of Columbus's 'discovery' of the Americas, Vasco da Gama was sailing around the Cape of Good Hope, to India.

Today, the achievements of Columbus and da Gama are often disparaged by the politically correct. I am not arguing that these were 'good' men. By modern standards, they clearly were not. However, there is no doubt that their extra-ordinary achievements were an integral part of the European revival. They represent the same spirit of adventure that drove Galileo and da Vinci.

In the last half century, Asia has gone through its own Renaissance and Industrial Revolution, rolled into one. What took centuries in Europe has happened in a few short decades.

India is now entering this phase. However, there is nothing inevitable about India's rise. Demographic change and growing literacy are but enabling factors. In the end, what matters is that India has the confidence to take advantage of the opportunity. This calls for a mental attitude that requires to be actively promoted. Human history is full of civilizational dead-ends and India's own history shows how things can unravel. The decline of Kolkata, the city of my birth, should serve as a warning that even the most cosmopolitan of societies can lose their way.

The Decline of Kolkata: A Cautionary Tale

At the beginning of the twentieth century, Calcutta (as it was known then) was the capital of the British empire in India. It was one of the most advanced and cosmopolitan cities in Asia. Its writ ran across the Indian subcontinent and Burma.[2] The city bustled with people from all over India and the world— Marwaris, Jews, Gujaratis, Armenians, Anglo-Indians were some of the communities that lived in this great metropolis. It even had a bustling Chinatown!

This does not mean that the native Bengalis were simply sidelined. The late nineteenth and early twentieth century were the high noon of Bengali culture. Led by stalwarts like Bankim Chandra, Sarat Chandra and Rabindranath Tagore, Bengali culture underwent a remarkable renaissance. Calcutta was the intellectual centre of both social reform and the struggle for independence from British rule. It had been home to Ram Mohan Roy, Vidyasagar, Swami Vivekananda, and Subhas Bose to name a few individuals that shaped modern India. In 1876, the Indian National Association, the first political organization of its kind, was set up in Calcutta by Surendranath Bannerjea. It would later evolve into the Congress party.

Even after the shift of the official capital to New Delhi in 1911 and the loss of part of its hinterland to East Pakistan in 1947, the city retained its position as the most important economic and cultural centre in the country. In 1950, the population of Calcutta's metropolitan area was 4.5 million compared to 2.9 million for Bombay and 1.4 million for Delhi.[3] Many of the country's top companies were headquartered in Calcutta and it was the preferred location for multinationals. The industrial cluster around Calcutta was the largest in Asia outside of Japan. This included a bustling port, British-era jute and textile mills as well as the 'modern' factories of Hindustan Motors (the producers of the Ambassador car), the Bata India Shoe Company and Chittaranjan Locomotive Works. The wealth and drive of the city were visible in the well-maintained colonial buildings of Chowringhee and the swinging nightlife of Park Street. As a cosmopolitan and energetic metropolis, no other Indian city came close.

Yet, today's Kolkata rarely merits a mention in the current economic boom. In the late-sixties it ceded its position as India's commercial capital to Mumbai, and has never made an attempt to regain this position. In terms of population, it is still the third-largest metropolitan area after Mumbai and Delhi but in terms of economic importance it would today count behind the likes of Bangalore, Hyderabad, Chennai and perhaps even Pune. What happened to the city is best illustrated by the story of Biren Mookerjee, known popularly as Sir Biren.

Sir Biren was the son of pioneer industrialist Rajen Mookerjee. After finishing his studies in England he returned to Calcutta in 1924. He quickly showed his business prowess and, by 1936, became the Chairman of the Steel Corporation of Bengal and was knighted in 1942. Then, following a merger, he came to head the Indian Iron and Steel Company (IISC), the second-largest steel manufacturer in the country. In the early years after Independence, Sir Biren was one of country's top corporate leaders. In 1953, he arranged for a US$31.5 million loan from the World Bank which was the first time that the agency had given a loan to a private company. The money was successfully used to modernize and expand capacity, and the loan was easily repaid. Till the mid-sixties, IISC was considered one of India's most dynamic companies.

All this changed within a few short years. A series of trade union strikes repeatedly shut down production between 1968 and 1972. Sir Biren tried to negotiate with the labour unions but wage demands were continuously hiked. This was ironical because IISC workers were then amongst the best paid in India. The disruptions pushed the company into a downward spiral and in 1972 it was taken over by the government. Sir Biren died a shattered man in 1982.

The IISC experience was hardly unique. From the late sixties, the industrial cluster around Calcutta was paralyzed by industrial action. Other industrial centres in the world faced trade union militancy in the sixties and seventies, but the situation in Calcutta was especially severe and prolonged. Well into the eighties, when I was a schoolboy, I remember often being stuck for hours in a crowded and sweltering bus due to road blocks set up by protesters. There were protests for higher pay, protest against computerization and other new technologies, protests against the Central government, protests against the 'Imperialist' policies of the United States. Not surprisingly, companies began to leave one by one. These included IT companies like IBM. But for this turn of events, it is quite likely that Calcutta rather than Bangalore would have been the centre of the services boom. Till the late sixties, it certainly had the best pool of white-collar workers in the country.

However, the decline was not just an economic one. What

happened to Calcutta in the last four decades is similar to what happened to India in the eleventh century. By the late sixties, Calcutta closed itself off, culturally and intellectually. Some may date the decline to the violent Naxalite movement of the late sixties, but it was a far wider malaise. Both the government and society at large turned increasingly against both private enterprise, innovation and new ideas.

Note that it was not just a matter of having a Communist-run government but a wider cultural attitude. Growing up in the city, I recall growing popular resentment against the economic success of minority groups like the Marwaris. Multinationals were virtually hounded, with popular support, out of the city. It was also with popular support that the authorities decided that the teaching of English was to be discontinued in government-controlled primary schools in an attempt to erase 'Imperialist influences'. Most absurd of all, there was a ban on any form of innovation in the way Rabindranath Tagore's works were represented. His songs and plays had to performed strictly according to formulae that were laid down from the top. Kolkata and Bengal had democratically elected to go backward.

The banning of English and of artistic innovation, of course, did not lead to a great renaissance of Bengali culture and literature. Quite to the contrary, Bengal has never again produced thinkers of the calibre of Rabindranath Tagore, Subhas Bose, Bankim Chandra, Satyajit Ray, Vivekananda and Raja Ram Mohan Roy. The discouragement of private enterprise also did not create a public-sector haven. Instead, public-sector companies like the State Bank of India shifted their headquarters to Mumbai in order to be near their private sector peers.

Some people may argue that the decline of the city is due to the long rule of the Communists. However, I think that it is a reflection of a deeper malaise that had begun to affect Indian attitudes from the fifties, and found its fullest expression in Bengal. The persecution of unorthodox intellectuals like Nirad Chaudhuri shows how Calcutta (and India) was becoming increasingly intolerant of self-criticism. In 1951, Nirad Chaudhuri publish his controversial *Autobiography of an Unknown Indian* where he criticized aspects of Indian culture and praised aspects of British rule. He argued that Indians, particularly Bengalis, were failing to maintain the intellectual standards of their nineteenth-century predecessors. In later writings, he even went so far as to accuse his contemporaries as having reduced Rabindranath Tagore to being 'the holy mascot of Bengali provincial vanity'.[4]

He not only attracted a barrage of criticism but was pushed out of his job at All India Radio and even denied a pension. There was a virtual ban on his works. Ultimately, he sought refuge in Oxford, England, where he died in 1999. Although I do not personally agree with all of Nirad Chaudhuri's views, his persecution shows how Indian, especially Bengali, openness to criticism had changed during the socialist era. In the end, it is this that caused the decline of Calcutta.

On a visit to the city in the late eighties, Prime Minister Rajiv Gandhi called it a 'dying city'. It caused much indignation amongst its citizens but it did not lead to a change in outlook. Rather than change policy, the state government concentrated on changing the names of well-known roads and streets. It eventually culminated in the renaming of Calcutta as Kolkata. Of course, this did not change anything. Faced with shrinking education and job opportunities, the once proud Bengali middle class (including me) has gradually shifted out to other parts of India and to the rest of the world. They were not exiled by foreign rule and persecution but by the lack of imagination.

Attitudes in the rest of India have changed since 1991 and

there are signs that things are slowly turning around even in Kolkata. The Communists still run the state but now they encourage investments from the rest of the world. After a lull of four decades, the city is witnessing new investments in areas such as real estate, infrastructure and IT. In a speech in January 2008, Chief Minister Buddhadeb Bhattacharya openly told his party cadres that there was no alternative to capitalism.[5] It's a pity that Sir Biren did not live to see the day. Of course, this is still work in progress and, as shown by the recent controversy over Bangladeshi writer Taslima Nasreen, there is some way to go. However, Calcutta—oops, sorry—Kolkata may yet live up to the ideals of Ram Mohan Roy, Vidyasagar and Tagore.

It should be pointed out, nevertheless, that cultural resistance to new ideas, outside influence and change is not exclusive to Kolkata, the Bengali people or to the political Left. Such sentiments can be found across the political spectrum and in many other parts of the country. Even in cosmopolitan Mumbai, we have recently seen sporadic attacks on 'outsiders', from the northern states of Uttar Pradesh and Bihar. Although these are still isolated events, the political leadership should recognize that Mumbai could yet meet with the fate of Kolkata if these incidents are not brought under control. The aspirations of the 'locals' must be fairly met but never by threatening the bubbling mix of peoples and influences that give the city its life.

In fact, the wider process of liberalization itself should not be taken for granted. At every stage there will always be a temptation to succumb to 'dead habit'. Even the champions of reform are susceptible to this. In 2004, the BJP-led government of Prime Minister Vajpayee was replaced by one led by the Congress and headed by Manmohan Singh, the very man who had initiated the liberalization process in 1991. His Cabinet included other well-known reformers such as Finance Minister

Chidambaram. There were expectations that India was about to embark on another round of tough reforms. Yet, the country saw few major initiatives in the years that followed. The economy continued to grow at a strong pace due to the cumulative impact of previous reforms but the policy regime stagnated. The few initiatives that the reformers proposed were struck down by the government's Communist allies.

Worse, as time wore on, the government itself proposed policies that echoed the failed ideas of the seventies and eighties. For instance, in February 2008, Finance Minister Chidambaram announced a massive debt-forgiveness programme for farm loans. No one is arguing that poor, indebted farmers should not be helped but there are many better ways of helping them. As previous experience shows, blanket debt-forgiveness only results in poor credit culture and eventually affects the long-term flow of resources to the rural community. Moreover, it does little to alleviate the problems of the truly needy because the poorest farmers are overwhelmingly indebted to local money lenders. Debt forgiveness in the formal banking system does little to help them and, if anything, is iniquitous. Surely, Prime Minister Singh and his Finance Minister knew this but they still succumbed to blatant populism. I felt personally let down.

Is the World Flat?

In his widely read book *The World is Flat*, Thomas Friedman argues that that the history of the twenty-first century will be about how technology and the wider process of globalization has created an interlinked world where geography does not matter. He talks about the 'Ten Forces that Flattened the Earth' including Supply-Chaining and Outsourcing. His central point is that the 'World is Flat' because it is now possible for anyone (presumably with the right skills) to participate in the world economy.

In a limited sense, Friedman is right. The communications revolution has indeed created a world where the anyone can pickup a phone or send an email to do business with anyone else in the world. However, it is not true that the process of globalization is new. It has been going on from the very beginning of history—well, at least since Sumerian ships unloaded their goods at the docks at Lothal. Moreover, it has not been a continuous uni-directional process. There have been periods of globalization followed by periods of isolation. India and China, both now at the forefront of Freidman's Flat Earth, are good examples of countries that had once globalized but then chose to close themselves. Similarly today, the opportunities of the Flat Earth are just as open to countries like Zimbabwe and North Korea but, so far, they have chosen not to take advantage of them.

The World is not Flat just because technology allows us to connect various points on the planet. The internet is no more than the latest step in a series of globalizing technologies that go back to the ships of the Spice Trade, the camel caravans of the Silk Route, the railways, telephones and the radio. To take advantage of the world, one needs the right attitude towards innovation, change and risk-taking. The real change in today's India is that there is a significant proportion of the population, the middle class, that feels confident and capable enough. The demographic shift and the primary education revolution will make it possible for more people to participate in the process in the near future. However, it is an opportunity that India still needs to actualize and its success will depend to a large extent on the choices it makes. As Columbus proved, the earth is not flat but round, and its opportunities are open only to those who dare to sail around it.

Asato Ma Sadgamaya,
Tamaso Ma Jyotirgamaya,
Mrtyor Ma Amritamgamaya

From Falsehood Unto Truth,
From Darkness Unto Light,
From Death Unto Immortality

—from the *Brihdaranyaka Upanishad,*
circa 9th century BC

Notes

1. Waiting for a Thousand Years

[1] The Portuguese held on to their enclaves in Goa, Daman and Diu till 1961, when they were forcibly evicted by Indian troops. They had been the first European colonial power in Asia and they were the last to leave. In 1999, they peacefully handed back Macau to China.

[2] The Indian diaspora first began to expand in the nineteenth century as groups of merchants and indentured labour began to settle in British colonies like Mauritius, South/East Africa, the Caribbean, Singapore and Fiji. By the nineteen-sixties, significant numbers moved to Britain and Canada (including refugees from Idi Amin's Uganda). From the seventies, the focus shifted to the United States which attracted large numbers of the country's most talented students. However, significant numbers also emigrated to the Gulf States. The latest trend shows Indian professions being attracted to rapidly growing cities like Dubai, Singapore and London.

[3] Some scholars are of the opinion that the civilization was centered along the now dry Saraswati river rather than the Indus. However, I have persisted with the term 'Indus Valley' as it is better known. In any case, the debate between the two rivers is not pertinent to this book.

4 Very little is known for sure about Chanakya but there are a number of strong legends and traditions related to him. His magnum opus, the *Arthashastra*, gives a good insight into the mind of this empire-builder.

5 Chapter on Trade and Transport Officials, *Arthashastra* by Kautilya.

6 No copy of *Indika* itself has survived but we have extensive quotes in the works of other Greek writers.

7 *The World Economy: Historical Statistics*, Angus Maddison, OECD 2003.

8 'Maritime Heritage of Orissa', Professor Atul Kr. Pradhan, Utkal University (paper taken from the Orissa government's official website).

9 This was not just a matter of trade protectionism. Gold was money, and the continuous outflow of gold was the ancient equivalent of severe monetary tightening.

10 This definition of the West does not include Eastern Europe and the USSR.

11 *The World Economy: Historical Statistics*, Angus Maddison, OECD 2003.

12 The English translation by John Briggs is available as the *History of Mahomedan Power in India* (reprinted in Sang-e-Meel Publications, New Delhi, 1981).

13 'The Mid-Eighteenth Century Background', by Tapan Raychaudhuri, Chapter 1 in *The Cambridge Economic History of India*, Vol. II, Cambridge University Press 2005 revised edition.

14 *Alberuni's India*, translated by Dr Edward Sachau, Rupa 2002.

15 *The Travels of Marco Polo* translated by Ronald Latham, Penguin 1958.

16 'Science and the Islamic World—the Quest for Rapprochement', Pervez Amirali Hoodbhoy, *Physics Today*, August 2007.

17 After the 'Golden Age' from the seventh to twelfth centuries,

the Muslim world too went into decline. In recent years, there has been some soul-searching amongst Muslim intellectuals about the causes of this decline. An interesting read in this context is Professor Pervez Amirali Hoodbhoy's article 'Science and the Islamic World—the Quest for Rapproachment', in *Physics Today*, August 2007.

18 *The Sanskrit Language*, Thomas Burrow, Faber & Faber (1955); *Rigvedic Loanwords*, F.B.J. Kuiper, in Studia Indologica (1955).

19 This may be somewhat inconvenient to modern-day Tamil purists who are attempting to remove Sanskrit-inspired words from Tamil.

2. From Independence to Freedom

1 *The Penguin Book of Modern Indian Speeches*, edited by Rakesh Batabyal, Penguin 2007.

2 *The Penguin Book of Modern Indian Speeches*, edited by Rakesh Batabyal, Penguin 2007.

3 Indeed, the Mughal empire began to unravel within a few decades after the completion of the Taj.

4 Between the reigns of Nehru and his daughter, the country was run briefly by Prime Minister Lal Bahadur Shastri (1964–66). He died unexpectedly in Tahskent in January 1966. Shastri was also had a socialist bent but was largely a pragmatist in matters of economic policy. Some people believe that India's economic trajectory would have been very different if he had survived.

5 This illustration of how the industrial licensing worked is taken from Chapter 17 of *Indian Economy Since Independence*, edited by Uma Kapila, 17th revised edition, 2006, Academic Foundation.

6 *Black Income in India*, Suraj B. Gupta, 1992 (page 146).

7 Readers interested in learning more about the series of

macroeconomic crises are directed to *India: Macroeconomics and Political Economy 1964–91*, by I.M.D. Little and Vijay Joshi, World Bank 1994.

8 Milton Friedman on the Nehru–Mahalnobis Plan, 15 February 1956, edited by Subroto Roy, 1998.

9 This book emphasizes Nehru's great errors because it focusses on economics. Nehru was a multifaceted man who also did many things right. The interested reader may read *Nehru: The Invention of India* by Shashi Tharoor for a different field of vision.

10 Rajni Kothari dubbed this as the 'Congress-system' although it has been hardly unique to state and Central regimes that run the Congress party. Even if one blames the Congress for providing the blueprint, other parties have developed and refined the system over the years.

11 *India After Gandhi*, by Ramchandra Guha, Picador 2007.

12 Chapter 11, in *India Unbound*, by Gurcharan Das, Penguin 2002 (revised edition).

13 This had been a pet project of Rajiv Gandhi's brother, the late Sanjay Gandhi.

14 The number related to 1980-81 to 1991-92—this period excludes the 1980 crisis but includes the growth impact of the 1991 crisis in order to fairly consider the impact of the policies of the 1980s.

15 For a discussion of this debate see 'The Growth Rate Mystery' by K.B.L. Mathur in *Indian Economy Since Independence*, edited by Uma Kapila 2006, 17th edition, published by Academic Foundation.

16 Those interested in the details of the academic debate over growth in the eighties are directed to 'India in the 1980s and 1990s: A triumph of Reforms', by Arvind Panagariya (Chapter 8), in *India's and China's Recent Experience with Reform and Growth*, edited by Wanda Tseng and David Cowen, IMF 2005.

[17] *The Penguin Book of Modern Indian Speeches*, edited by Rakesh Batabyal, Penguin 2007.
[18] *The Penguin Book of Modern Indian Speeches*, edited by Rakesh Batabyal, Penguin 2007.
[19] A good account of this unwillingness is given by Gurcharan Das in his book *India Unbound* (chapter 15), Penguin 2002.

3. The Entrepreneurial Explosion

[1] *India Today*, 31 March 1992.
[2] IT Asia Millennium Lecture, 29 November 2000.
[3] 'The Impact Economic Reforms in India: A case study of the Software Industry' by Narayana Murthy, in *India's Emerging Economy*, edited by Kaushik Basu, OUP, 2004.
[4] For a more detailed discussion of these events read *The Backroom Brigade*, by Seetha, Penguin Portfolio 2006.
[5] 'From Hindu Growth to Productivity Surge: The Mystery of Indian Growth Transition', Arvind Subramanium and Dani Rodrik, NBER Working Paper, March 2004.
[6] GSM plus CDMA.
[7] Nasscom estimates.
[8] The Sensex peaked at crossed 20,000 by December 2007. This was the highest it had reached at the time of writing.
[9] 'India's Pattern of Development: What Happened and What Follows?', Raghuram Rajan et al., IMF Working Paper, January 2006.
[10] Note that agriculture here includes other primary activities like mining, fishing and quarrying. Industry includes construction and utilities in addition to manufacturing.
[11] 'India's Pattern of Development: What Happened, What Follows?', Raghuram Rajan et al., IMF Working Paper, January 2006.
[12] Of course, railway technology itself is seeing a dramatic improvement and the sector may well see a come back.

However, it will be completely different mode of transport—
far removed from the trundling trains of the past.

13 Admittedly, China is perhaps the most extreme example of the
'conventional' growth path.

14 There are instances where outdated laws did impinge on the
emerging services sector. There is the infamous instance when
it was deemed illegal to employ women in night-shifts at call-
centre industry in Gurgaon! However, these are minor hurdles
compared to those faced by employers in manufacturing.

15 *The World is Flat* by Thomas Friedman, published by Penguin
2007.

4. The Great Indian Middle Class and Its Limitations

1 The resurrection of Hebrew in modern Israel is an example of
how an ancient language can be brought alive again. However,
it may not have been a practical idea in a large and diverse
country like India, especially during a period of colonial rule.

2 Syama Prasad Mookerjee founded the Bharatiya Jana Sangh in
1951. This would evolve into the party today called the
Bharatiya Janata Party. This quote is taken from the *Penguin
Book of Modern Indian Speeches*, 2007.

3 Shashi Tharoor once pointed out this trend in his column—
'Save the Sari from a Sorry Fate', 24 May 2007, *Times of
India*. His article triggered a big debate. Clearly a lot of Indian
women feel strongly about this issue.

4 *India Today*, 19 June 2006.

5 *The Economist*, 6–13 August 2006.

6 'Indian docs in UK returning home to better hospitals', *The
Straits Times*, 17 December 2007.

7 'The Respect they Deserve', Gurcharan Das, Viewpoint, *Time*,
Asia edition, 29 November 2004.

8 'The "Bird of Gold": The Rise of India's Consumer Market',
McKinsey Global Institute, May 2007.

[9] Tata Statistical Outline of India 2005-06.

[10] 'Time for India's IT outsourcers to take a fresh look at the data', Joe Leahy, *Financial Times*, 28 December 2007.

5. Poverty, Inequality and the Last Bastion of Control

[1] *Data and Dogma: The Great Indian Poverty Debate*, Angus Deaton and Valerie Kozel, OUP, 2005.

[2] 'Unemployment & Wages: Ideology, Reforms and Evidence', Surjit Bhalla and Tirthamoy Das, Oxus Research (paper presented at the India Policy Forum Conference July 2005).

[3] Table 1.A1.3 Panel B, OECD Employment Outlook 2007

[4] 'Agricultural Productivity, Rural Diversity & Economic Reforms: India 1970-2000,' October 2003 and 'Agricultural Development, Industrialization & Rural Inequality', April 2004. Both are internet versions.

[5] 'Farm Sector Performance and the Reform Agenda', Rip Landes and Ashok Gulati, in' Indian Economy Since Independence' edited by Uma Kapila, Academic Foundation 2006.

[6] 'Development, Democracy and the Village Telephone', by Sam Pitroda, Harvard Business Review, November–December 1993.

[7] 'The Digital Provide: Information (Technology), Market Performance and Welfare in the South Indian Fisheries Sector', Robert Jensen, Quarterly Journal of Economics, August 2007.

[8] 'The Other MIT', *Business Week*, 22 May, 2005.

[9] These cities are now known as Kolkata, Mumbai and Chennai—but I have used the old names here as they were used during colonial period.

[10] 'Higher Education in India: The Need for Change', Pavan Agarwal, ICRIER Working Paper, June 2006.

[11] 'Framing the Engineering Outsourcing Debate: Placing the US on a Level Playing Field with China and India', Gary Gereffi & Vivek Wadhwa, Duke University, December 2005.

[12] Estimates from Pavan Agarwal (2006).

[13] *Ensuring India's Offshoring Future*, Diana Farrel, Noshir Kaka and Sascha Sturze, McKinsey 2005.

[14] *Times of India*, 21 March 2005.

[15] 'Higher Education in India: Seizing the Opportunity', Sanat Kaul, ICRIER Working Paper, May 2006.

[16] Mother Teresa did win the Nobel Prize for Peace in 1979 but surely she cannot be presented as a success for India's education system.

[17] In recent years, the Education Ministry has been renamed as Human Resource Development Ministry—with a slightly wider mandate.

[18] Table A24 in Pavan Agarwal (2006).

[19] 'Absence of Policy and Perspective in Higher Education', J.B.G. Tilak, *Economic and Political Weekly*, 22 May 2004.

[20] This attitude has caused a great deal of damage in other countries as well. Notice how high-quality staff and students have steadily drifted away from European institutions to US universities.

[21] 'The Mess in Education', Ajay Shah, *Business Standard*, 28 February 2006.

[22] An institution called the National Assessment and Accreditation Council does exist but it has not been a great success. It was established in 1994 and it took till 1998 to accredit its first institution. The pace has picked up in recent years but it has mostly stuck to assessing government and government-aided institutions.

[23] 'China Model for Higher Education, says Pranab', *Hindustan Times*, 12 September 2007.

6. Two Revolutions

[1] *The World Economy*, Angus Maddison, OECD 2001.

[2] UN Population Statistics— http://www.un.org/popin/data.html

[3] Ibid.

[4] Some economists think that the life-cycle is supposed to only influence household savings rates rather than national savings rates. However, this is an artificial distinction as corporate savings eventually accrue to shareholders (i.e. households) just as public savings eventually reflects in future taxes/subsidies to citizens. Thus the split between the various types of savings is just a matter of portfolio choice and institutional structure. This is a kind of Ricardian Equivalence. The lifecycle, therefore, affects overall savings in the economy and not just household savings.

[5] 'Demographic Transitions and Economic Miracles in Emerging Asia', by David Bloom and Jeffrey Williamson, NBER WP6268, November 1997.

[6] 'Longevity and Life Cycle Savings' by David Bloom, David Canning, and Bryan Graham, NBER WP8808, Mar 2002.

[7] It appears that the investment–savings peak is somewhat before the actual demographic peak. We are not sure why this is the case. Possibly, the activity begins to cool off once economic agents feel more comfortable with the newly acquired savings pool and production capacity.

[8] 'Domestic Savings and International Capital Flows', Martin Felstein & Charles Horioka, *Economic Journal*, June 1980.

[9] 'Private Schools for the Poor: A Case Study from India', James Tooley and Pauline Dixon, CfBT Research and Development, 2003.

[10] 'Public and Private Schools in Rural India' by Karthik Murlidharan & Michael Kremer, March 2006, Department of Economics, Harvard University.

[11] 'Teach Me English', John Kurrien, *Times of India* editorial, 8 October 2006.

[12] 'The Myth of Asian Miracle' by Paul Krugman, *Foreign Affairs*, November–December 1994.

[13] *Early Modern Gloucester (upto 1640): Religious & Cultural Life* (Volume 4), Victoria County History, 1988.

[14] 'Paths to Lower Fertility', John Caldell, *British Medical Journal*, October 1999.

[15] 'The Protestant Work Ethic and the Spirit of Capitalism', Max Weber, 1905.

[16] *Lands and Peoples*, Volume IV, Grolier Society, 1956 edition.

[17] 'Here Come the Jobs', T.N. Ninan, *Business Standard*, 7 November 2006.

[18] 'DLF to bring home 20,000 migrant workers', *Economic Times*, 5 November 2007; '1.62 Lakh Vacancies in Railways', *Times of India*, 3 November 2007.

7. The Importance of Institutional Reform

[1] An earlier version of this chapter was presented at the 'Conference on Governance' organized by the India Development Foundation on 7–9 August 2006 at Taj Mansingh, New Delhi.

[2] The *Arthashastra* considered the provision of public order as one of the main functions of the State. Similarly, Adam Smith argued that laws were means through which the State promotes public prosperity.

[3] See *Lawlessness and Economics* by Avinash Dixit, Princeton University Press 2004; and *Trust: Social Virtues and the Creation of Prosperity* by Francis Fukuyama, Penguin 1995.

[4] See 'Chinese Legal Reform at the Crossroads', Jerome Alan Cohen, *Far Eastern Economic Review*, March 2006.

[5] See *The Future of India: Politics, Economics and Governance* by Dr Bimal Jalan, Penguin 2005.

[6] 'Judicial Reform—law and contract enforcement', Bibek Debroy (undated internet version, www.mayin.org).

[7] Report of the Commission on Review of Administrative Laws, September 1998.

[8] 'Reforming the Legal System', Bibek Debroy (undated internet version, www.mayin/ajayshah/A/Debroyl.pdf).

[9] Civil law traditions deal with old laws through the doctrine of 'Desuetude' by which laws are deemed outdated and unenforceable if they have not been actively enforced for a long time.

[10] Beedis are Indian-style cigarettes made from tendu leaves.

[11] The author was unable to trace the original Law Ministry statement.

[12] Bharat Forge Co. Ltd. Vs Uttam Manohar Nakate 2005.

[13] '14 years in courts, 1 hour to walk free', Rukmini Srinivasan, *Times of India*, 27 March 2008.

[14] *The Mystery of Capital: Why Capitalism Triumphs in the West and Fails Everywhere Else*, Hernando de Soto, Basic Books 2000.

[15] 'Nandigram turns Blood Red', *Economic Times*, 15 March 2007.

8. How India Will Change

[1] World Urbanization Prospects 2005, UN.

[2] The only notable exception is Ambedkar who saw Indian villages as caste-ridden hierarchies that inhibited development.

[3] World Urbanization Prospects, The 2007 Revision, UN, February 2008.

[4] 'Was the Industrial Revolution inevitable? Economic Growth over the very long run', Charles Jones, NBER Working Paper, October 1999.

[5] It could be argued that the Dutch shared this with the British, but that the Britain surged ahead because it was large enough (and insulated from Continental wars) to hit the critical mass of investment needed to trigger the Industrial Revolution.

[6] *Second Among Equals: the Middle Class Kingdoms of India and China*, Surjit Bhalla, Peterson Institute of International Economics (forthcoming).

[7] The Venetian republic developed remarkably modern market-

institutions in the late Middle Ages. This allowed the city-state to remain a major economic power over six centuries and made it a leading centre of the Renaissance.

8 Quoted from the section called 'Letter to Monseigneur Colbert: Concerning Hindustan'.

9 'Markets in China and Europe on the Eve of the Industrial Revolution'—Carol Shields, University of Texas, August 2004.

10 *The Great Indian Middle Class*, by Pavan Varma, Penguin 1998.

11 *Second Among Equals: The Middle Class Kingdoms of India and China*, Surjit S. Bhalla, Peterson Institute of International Economics (forthcoming).

12 'For Korean Middle Class, a Process of Politicization', Susan Chira, *New York Times*, 19 June 1987. 'Korean Middle Class Agonizes over Vote', Susan Chira, *New York Times*, 14 December 1987.

13 Of course, this comment should be seen in the context of the times. Mahatma Gandhi was more than open to Western ideas when it suited his cause.

14 *India After Gandhi*, Ramchandra Guha, Picador India 2007.

15 Regional languages remain strong and local popular culture is more than alive despite the pan-Indian attractions of Hindi. This is especially true in the southern-most states.

16 'Career, not caste, clicks for web knots', Neha Mehta, 2 December 2007, *Hindustan Times*.

17 'As China Roars, Pollution Reaches Deadly Extremes', *New York Times* Special Series 'Choking on Growth', Part 1, 26 August 2007.

18 'China Green National Accounting Study Report 2004' published by NBS, September 2006.

19 For those interested in the Green Accounting for Indian States Project, look for publications in the website: www.gistindia.org. Note that the methodology and scope is different from the Chinese approach and the two are not strictly comparable.

[20] 'Accounting for Fresh Water Quality in India', GAISP Monograph 8, by Pushpam Kumar, Sanjeev Sanyal, Rajiv Sinha & Pavan Sukhdev, Teripress 2007.

[21] *How Societies Choose to Fail and Succeed*, Jared Diamond, Penguin, 2004.

[22] A new PPP estimate for 2005 was published just as this book was going to print. I have deliberately omitted it as it used a new methodology that does not give comparable numbers for the past.

[23] 'Dancing with Giants' edited by Alan Winters and Shahid Yusuf, World Bank 2006.

[24] 'Indian soap operas "addiction" in Afghanistan', by Sayad Salahuddin, Reuters, 18 May 2006.

9. Is India's Rise Inevitable?

[1] *The Renaissance*, Paul Johnson, Phoenix Press, 2000.

[2] It may come as some surprise to some that Singapore was set up and run for decades by the Bengal Civil Service.

[3] 'Urban India: Understanding the Maximum City', Urban Age 2007.

[4] 'Obituary: Nirad C. Chaudhury', *The Independent* (London), 3 August 1999.

[5] 'No alternative to Capitalism now', *The Hindu*, 4 January 2008.

Index

Abdul Gaffar, 158
Aden, 18, 20
Aditya Birla Group, 60, 144
adulteration, 34
affirmative action, 108
Afghanistan, 192; Taliban rule, 62, 63
Afghans, 14, 175
agricultural sector, 72, 76, 102–04, 140, 143; productivity, 104; share in economy, 74, 102; subsistence agriculture, 122, 130
Ahmed Shah Abdali, 175
Ahoms of Assam, 16
Air Corporation Act (1953), 54
airline industry, 54–55, 74, 91
Akbar, 17, 25
Alexander, 6
Alexandria, 9; library, 21, 194
All India Council for Technical Education (AICTE), 115
Ambani, Dhirubhai, 54, 88
Ambassador car, 35
American Express, 65–66
Angkor (Cambodia), 8, 12
Ansal Plaza, 69
Arabic, 25, 82
Arabs, 19
Arthashastra, 6, 149, 206n⁴

Aryabhatta, 10, 25
Aryan Invasion theory, 6
Asia Satellite Telecommunications, 57
Asian Crisis (1997), 61, 63, 71, 135, 137, 146, 164
Asian Games, Delhi (1982), 44
Asian growth miracle/development experience, 128, 135, 139, 164, 178, 188–89
AsiaSat, 57
Assamese, 23
automobile industry, 138, 189; exports, 71
Awami League, 41

Bactrians, 15
Bahujan Samaj Party (BSP), 177
Bajajs, 54, 60
balance-of-payment (BoP) crisis, 47, 58
Bali, 8, 9
Bangladesh, 40, 42
Bankim Chandra, 197, 200
banking sector, 54, 61, 67, 69, 91, 128–29
Bannerjea, Surendranath, 197
Bappa Rawal, 16
Bar Council of India, 115

Bata India Shoe Company, 198
beedi industry, legislations, 154–55
Bengali, 23, 25, 26, 82; middle class, 201
Berlin wall, fall, 46–47
Bernier, Francois, 174
Al-Beruni, 17, 83
Bhakra Nangal dam cum irrigation system, 31
Bharat Forge, 68, 157
Bharati, 144
Bharatiya Janata Party (BJP), 47, 52, 62–63, 86
Bhatia, Sabeer, 65
Bhattacharya, Buddhadeb, 161, 202
Bihar: education, 113, 133
Birlas, 54
black marketing, 35, 89–90. See also corruption
Bollywood, 191–93
Bose, Sarat Chandra, 197
Bose, Subhas Chandra, 84, 197, 200
bribery and rent-seeking, 154, 172. See also corruption
Britain. See United Kingdom
British Airways, 66
British Broadcasting Corporation (BBC), 57
Bronze Age civilizations, 6
Buddhism, 7, 12, 110
bureaucracy, bureaucratic control, 28, 29, 34, 39–40, 55, 77, 85, 88, 170
Byzantines, 15

Cable News Network (CNN), 57
cable television, 57–58, 73, 119
Calcutta University, 26
call-centre outsourcing business, 92–93, 155

Cape of Good Hope, 20
capital mobility, 128
capitalism, 149
caste-based organizations/networks, 31, 150
Champa, Hindu kingdom, 8
Chandragupta Maurya, 6
Chandrashekhar, S., 47, 114
Charaka, 25
Charles I, 172
Charles II, 172
Chatterjee, Somnath, 50
Chhattisgarh Private Universities Act, 118
Chaudhuri, Nirad C., 201
Chenery, 72
Chengiz Khan Operation, 41
Chetty, Gazulu, 26
Chidamabarm, P., 52, 59
child labour, 101
China, 19, 137–38, 164; Cultural Revolution, 90; demographic shifts, 126, 134, 188; economy, 13, 14, 70–72, 75, 186–89; export markets, 188; gross domestic product (GDP), 72, 75, 128–29, 185; higher education, 46, 111–12, 113, 116; integration, 189; investment boom, 129; manpower shortage, 94; Mao's revolution (1949), 49; middle class, 90; naval technology, 20–21; 'One Child Policy', 123, 188; pollution, 184, 185; printing techniques, 136, 195; urbanization, 165–66
Chittaranjan Locomotive Works, 198
Chola empire, 11, 18
Chhota Nagpur Encumbered Estates Act, 1875, 153
Christian armies, 19

Christian Church, 21
civil aviation sector, 73, 119–20
civil services, 78, 84, 176
Clive, Robert, 176
colonization, 3, 4, 23, 110
Columbus, Christopher, 20, 196, 204
Common Era, 13
communications revolutions, 203
Communist Party of India (Marxist) (CPI-M), 161
Communists, 29, 43, 120, 200, 201
competition, 57, 60, 88, 108, 115, 117, 120, 189
computerization, 199
Congress, 27, 28, 38, 40, 42, 50, 59, 84
Constitution of India, 115, 154
consumer class, 138
contraceptives, 123
contracts, enforcing, 160
Copernicus, Nicholas, 10
corruption and inefficiency, 35, 46, 59, 89–90, 170
Corus, 68
Council of Architects, 115, 116
credit card business, 65, 69. See also banking sector
creditworthiness, 33
Cromwell, Oliver, 172
Crossroads, 69
cultural traditions, 3, 9, 11–12, 191; modernization, 26; openness, 193

DLF, 144–45
da Gama, Vasco, 20, 196
da Vinci, Leonardo, 195
Dailmer Chrysler, 68
Damania Airlines, 54
Danish trade in India, 24

Dark Ages, 194–95
Delhi University, 77, 111, 116
de-licensing and deregulation, 99, 148
Delimitation Commission of India, 179
democratization, 136; of knowledge, 196
demographic shift, 3–4, 87, 123–27, 129, 139, 142–43, 145–46, 197; impact on economic performance, 127, 134. See also population growth
Deng Xiaoping, 49
Deve Gowda, H.D., 59, 62
Dhofar, 18
Diclofenac, 184–85
Distance Education Councils, 116
domestic savings, 75, 130; impact of demographic shift, 127–28
domestic sectors, 54, 91
Doordarshan (DD), 56, 154
Dravidian language, 23
Duke of Norfolk, 173

East and West ancient trade, 8–10
East India Company, 24, 42, 176, 190
East-West Airlines, 54
ecological biology, 29
economic: change, 67; development/growth, 36, 80, 98, 140, 165–66, 170, 185; policies, 128; powers, 190–91; reform process (1980s), 43–46;— (1991), 48–50, 73, 163. See also liberalization of economy; renaissance, 194; system, 27, 85, 137, 147, 151
economy, 12–13, 29, 31–32, 35–36, 38–39, 44–45, 59, 72–75, 117, 122–23, 134, 137, 160; of

ancient India, 7–8
education, 25–26, 30, 82–86, 88,
94, 102, 108–10, 116–17, 123,
133, 139, 143, 145, 148;
examination system, 86, 89, 112;
government investment, 116–17;
government-run schools, 132–
33; higher education, 108–11,
115–16, 180;—problems, 111–
14; illiteracy, 122, 131;
individual investment, 117–18;
literacy rate, 4, 46, 130–31, 134–
35, 145–46; market driven, 118;
primary education revolution,
130–34; private schools, 132;
school enrollment rates, 101,
142
Emergency (1975–77), 42, 123
employment: employability, 112,
145; generation capacity, 142–
46; growth, 100; relevance of
higher education system, 113
English Civil War (1642–51), 172
English education, 25–26, 84–86,
88, 110, 181–82, 200
Enron, 59
entertainment industry, 192–93
entrepreneurship, 17, 22, 35, 49,
145
entrepreneurial explosion, 52*ff*, 97,
98, 129; first phase (1992–97),
53–59; second phase (1998–
2002), 59–66; third phase
(2003–), 66–70
environment cost of development,
184–86
Europe, European, 19, 24; colonial
powers, 14, 16, 20; demographic
shift, 136–37; economy, 13–14;
industrialization, 176;
Renaissance, 136, 182, 194
European Union (EU), 184

exchange rate, 49
expatriate community, 191–92
exports, 19, 71

Fabian socialism, 31
Factories Act (1948), 153, 154
family institutions, 183
feudal power-structures, 172, 174
Fiat, 35
financial sector, 93, 137, 143;
government control, 55
fishing industry, 106
forced sterilization, 123
Ford, 190
Foreign Education Providers Bill,
120
foreign exchange reserves, 47–49,
58, 70
foreign institutional investors (FIIs),
53
Freedom Movement. *See*
independence movement
French Revolution, 172
Fust, Johann, 195

Galbraith, John Kenneth, 37
Galileo, 10, 21, 195, 196
Gandhi, Feroz, 39
Gandhi, Indira, 27, 32, 39, 40,
41–43, 44, 176
Gandhi, M.K., 28, 38, 50, 84,
167, 181
Gandhi, Rajiv, 44–45, 48, 105,
201
Gandhi, Sanjay, 208n[13]
General Electric (GE), 66
geo-politics, 40–43
global services trade, 92
globalization, 78–79, 98, 202–03
golden past, 5–12; decline, 12–
14;—reasons of, 14–20
'Golden Quadrilateral' road
project, 67

governance, 118, 170, 186; and second generation reforms, 147–49. *See also* bureaucracy. state government control. *See* bureaucratic control. *See also* licensing
Great Depression, 137
Great Leap Forward, 90
Greeks, 6, 7, 17, 83, 182
Green Revolution, 46, 101–02, 104
gross domestic product (GDP), 36, 43, 44, 58, 69–70, 75, 97, 98, 129–30, 139, 143, 163, 187; share of farm sector, 102; World GDP, Indian share, 186
Gujral, Inder Kumar, 62
Gulf War I (1990), 47, 57
Gupta empire, 10, 15
Gutenburg, Johann, 195

hard versus soft power, 190–93
Harvard College, 173
heavy engineering, 138
higher education. *See* education
Hindi, 23, 85–86
Hindu Shahi kings, 16
Hinduism, Hindus, 7, 12
Hindustan Motors, 35, 198
Hippalus, 8
Hollywood, 191, 192
Honda, 68
Hong Kong, 164
Hormuz, 18
Hotmail, 65
housing, gradation, 86–87
Hum Log, 56
human capital, 77, 92, 94, 174
human history, 197
Huns, 15
Hypatia, 21

IBM, 199
Iberian peninsula, 15, 19

Ibn Batuta, 18
illiteracy. *See* education
Iltutmish, Sultan, 110
import-substitution, 30, 36, 38–40
income tax, 33
income, per capita, 13, 73, 188
independence: and after, 84–90; to freedom, 28*ff*; movement, 26, 87, 176
Indian Airlines flight hijacked, 1999, 63
Indian civilization, decline, 14–20
Indian Growth model, 70–79, 107
Indian Institutes of Management (IIMs), 77, 91, 111
Indian Institutes of Technology (IITs), 64, 77, 85, 111, 114
Indian Iron and Steel Company (IISC), 198–99
Indian National Association (INA), 197
Indian Ocean, 19, 20, 174; maritime network, 8
Indian Telegraph Act, 1885, 154
Indo-Arab mathematics, 136
Indo-Greeks, 15
Indonesia (Majapahit), 8, 9, 12; democracy, 180; literacy rate, 46; urbanization, 165
Indus Valley Civilization, 5–6, 167, 186
Industrial Development Bank of India (IDBI), 32
Industrial Disputes Act (1947), 154
Industrial Policy Resolution (1956), 28–29; (1977), 43; 1991, 53
Industrial Revolution, industrialization, 12–14, 80–81, 83, 136, 165, 167, 171–72, 173, 174, 184, 190, 196
industrial sector, 48, 67, 72, 73,

76, 174; restructuring, 61–67, 72, 101
industrial townships, 86
inequality and unemployment, 107–10
infant mortality, 46
inflation, 69
Information and Broadcasting Ministry, 57
information technology (IT) industry, 64–65, 68–69, 73, 96–97, 202; Enabled Services (ITES), 65, 68, 97
Infosys, 64, 73, 90
infrastructure: institutional, 170; physical, 59, 66–67, 70, 72, 122, 139–42; spending, 76
INSAT, 56
institutional: egos, 116; framework, 149, 176, 179; reforms, 147*ff*; structure, 169
intellectual leadership, 20, 24, 26
interest rates, 69, 75
International Monetary Fund (IMF), 48, 51, 73
international trading network, 187, 190
internationalization, 71
investment boom, 128
Islam, 182
Islamic civilization, 19

Jaguar, 190
Jain Commission, 153
Jalan, Bimal, 151
James II, 172
Janata Party, 42–43; government collapse (1979), 43
Japan, 36, 71, 137; demographic shifts, 125–26, 134; economy, 188, 189; Meiji Restoration, 3, 4; urbanization, 165

Jats, 175
Java (Yavadwipa), 8, 191
Jawaharlal Nehru University, Delhi, 116
Jessica Lall murder case, 158–59, 179
Jet Airways, 54, 55
Jews, 11
Jinnah, Muhammad Ali, 84
job opportunities, job market, 90, 93, 177
judicial system, *See* legal system
Justinian, 21

Kais, 18
Kalidasa, 23
Kalyani, Baba, 68
Kargil war (1999), 62–63
Kautilya (Chankya), 6–7, 149
Khilji, Bakhtiyar, 110
Khmer Rouge, 41
Khorana, Hargobind, 114
Khosla, Vinod, 65
Khurasan, 17
Kohli, Faqir Chand, 64
Kolkata, decline, 197–202
Krishi Darshan, 56
Krishnadeva Raya, 17
Krishnamachari, T.T., 39
Kuznets, 72

labour force, 122; unrest, 61
labour laws, 61, 77, 154–55, 157
Lahiri, Jhumpa, 182
Land Rover, 190
language issue, 85–86, 181–82
Latin, 22, 83
Law Commissions, 162
Lee Kuan Yew, 37
legal system (justice system, judiciary), 84, 146, 150–51, 154, 156–57, 162, 163, 176, 180; enforcement of rules, 156–60;

infrastructure, 152, 160–61; role, 149–52; old and dysfunctional, 153–54; in post-liberalization State, 160; reforms, 160–63; system of Appeals, 162; witness protection mechanism, 159

Lepers Act, 1898, 153

liberalization: of banking sector, 117; of economy, 1–2, 12, 35, 45, 47, 50–51, 52–54, 58, 60, 61, 66–67, 70–71, 77–78, 90, 98–99, 107, 112, 118, 129, 137, 142, 148, 170, 177; of education, 120; and rural India, 101–07; and telecommunications, 106

licensing system, 33, 35, 48, 60, 88, 115

Life Insurance Corporation of India (LIC), 32, 39

literacy rate. *See* education

London University, 111

MTV, 57

Macaulay, Thomas B., 82

Mahabharata, 23, 56

Mahalanobis, Prashanta Chandra, 2, 4, 29–37, 45, 58, 77, 85, 100, 112, 123; failure of vision, 37–40

Mahindra & Mahindra, 60

Mahmud of Ghazni, 4, 14, 17

Malabar coast, 20

Malacca, 20

Malaysia, 9

Manipal Institute of Technology, 120

manpower shortages, 92–94

manufacturing sector, 7, 64, 70–73, 122, 130, 137, 143–44, 187–89; share in GDP, 73

Maoist rebellions, 161

Marathas, 175

maritime trade, 10, 18

market, market-based economic system, 54, 76, 146, 148–49, 160, 176–77; capitalization, 114; uncertainty, 106

Marshall, John, 168

Maruti 800, 44–45

Maruti Udyog Limited, 44

Masani, Minoo, 38

mass media, 54, 179

Matto, Priyadarshani, murder case, 179

Mauryan empire, 6, 7, 15

McKinsey Global Institute, 65, 178

Medical Council of India, 115

Medicis, 195

Megasthenes, 7

Mehta, Harshad, 58–59

Meluhha, 6

mergers and acquisitions, 68

Mesopotamia, 5

metro-rail systems, 169

Michelangelo, 195

middle class, 4, 79, 136, 138–39, 145, 167, 176–77, 180, 182; educated, 81–86, 88, 94, 99, 108–11, 120, 122, 133, 143, 167; growth model based on, 123; and institutional change, 170–80; limitations, 80ff; in politics, 178–79; urban, 84, 133, 170, 178–79, 181, 183, 181; white-collar jobs, 107

Middle-East, 19, 21

military power, 190–91

military technology, 16

Millennium India Deposit, 63

mindset shift, 91

Mirzapur Stone Mahal Act, 1886, 153

mobile telephones, 91, 106, 120
modernization, 183
ModiLuft Airlines, 54
Mongols, 14, 19
Monopolies and Restrictive Trade Practices (MRTP) Act, 1969, 35, 48, 53, 64
Mookerjee, Biren, 198–99, 202
Mookerjee, Shyma Prasad, 86
Mughal empire, Muslim conquest of India, 14–16, 19, 24, 83, 174–75; disintegration, 25
Muhammad Ghori, 14
multinational companies (MNCs), 68, 90–91, 190
Munda, 23
Mundhra Scandal (1957), 39
Murdoch, Rupert, 57
Murthy, Narayana, 64, 65, 90
Muzaris, 8

NDTV, 90
Nadir Shah, 175
Naipaul, V.S., 15
Nakate, Uttam, 157–58
Nalanda, 11, 110
Nandigram, 160–61
Nano, 188
Naoroji, Dadabhai, 26
Napoleon Bonaparte, 172–73
Narasimha Rao, P.V., 48–51, 52
Nasreen, Taslima, 202
national consciousness, 84
National Council for Agricultural Research, 115
National Democratic Alliance (NDA), 63
National Institute of Information Technology (NIIT), 73, 119
National Knowledge Commission, 120
nationalization, 33

Naxalite movement, 200
Nehru, Jawaharlal, 2, 4, 27, 28, 30–31, 35, 37–39, 43, 45, 46, 49, 50, 58, 60, 84, 123, 181
Newly Industrialized Countries, 164
Newton, Isaac, 29
Nikator, Seleucus, 6
nineteenth-century re-awakening, 24–27
Nixon, Richard M., 41–42
non-farm activities, 102–03
non-governmental organizations (NGOs), 132
North Atlantic Treaty Organization (NATO), 192
nuclear test (1998), 62

Oil Shock, 43
openness culture, 20–22, 37, 55
Oudh Talukdars Relief Act (1870), 163
outsourcing, 63, 66, 71, 155, 203
over-regulation, 23–24, 76, 116
Oxford University, 110

PL-480, 46
Pakistan: Indian response to East disturbances, 41–42; military dictatorship, 40; West, 40–41
Panini, 23
Parsis, 11, 17
Partition of the Indian subcontinent, 1
Patanjali, 23
Patel, Sardar Vallabhbhai, 38
Pawar, Rajendra, 119
Persian, 25, 82, 83
pharmaceuticals, 138
Pharmacy Council of India, 116
Pitroda, Sam, 105, 120
Planning Commission, 29
Plassey Battle (1757), 24

Plato, 21
Pliny, 9
Pol Pot, 41
politics, 170, 176–77;
    consciousness, 176;
    considerations, 62, 147, 179;
    economy, 6, 39; leadership, 33,
    202; refugees, 12; uncertainty,
    62
Polo, Marco, 8, 17, 18
population growth, 123–27, 129,
    139, 144. *See also* demography
Portuguese, 20, 24
poverty, 160, 165; inequality and
    the last bastion of control, 98*ff*;
    and jobless growth, 99–101
Prakrits, 22, 23, 182
Premier Automobiles, 35
Premji, Azim, 64, 65
Presidency College, Kolkata, 82
printing technology, 136, 195–96
    private sector, 4, 28, 29, 32–34,
    37, 43, 54, 57, 59, 60, 70, 86,
    91, 117; banks, 55; education,
    118–20
privatization, 148. *See also*
    liberalization
professional councils, 115
property rights, 160, 170
Protestant Work Ethic, 137
Public Call Operators (PCOs), 105
Public Distribution System (PDS),
    33
public opinion, 159
public sector, 30–32, 35, 37, 43,
    48–49, 60, 72, 73, 85, 88–89,
    91, 99, 104, 130, 148, 175, 177
public transport networks, 169
Punjab Shops and Commercial
    Establishments Act, (1958), 155
Purchasing Power Parity (PPP), 95,
    186

quantitative controls, 54

railroad mileage, 141
railway system, railways, 73–74,
    145
Rajagopalachari, Chakravarti, 38,
    42, 181
Rajasthan: education, 131, 133
Rajputs of Mewar, 16
Raju, S.V., 42
Rakesh Mohan, 61
Raman, C.V., 114
Ramayana, 9, 23, 56, 191
Ranade, Madhav, 26
Rashtriya Janata Dal (RJD), 177
Ray, Satyajit, 200
Red Sea, 9
Reliance, 54, 144, 145
religious practices, 84
religious vigour theory, 16
Reserve Bank of India (RBI), 48,
    61, 86, 152, 163
resource allocation, government
    control, 32, 55
Resurgent India Bonds, 63
retail sector, 138, 143
Rig Veda, 23
Right to Information Act (RTI),
    179
risk-taking and innovation, 29, 31,
    49, 136, 170, 194–95
Robinson, John, 37
Roman Catholic, 22
Roman Empire, 7, 9–10, 13, 21,
    194
Romans, 11, 182
Roy, Prannoy, 90
Roy, Raja Ram Mohun, 2, 25–26,
    82–84, 109, 181, 197, 200, 202
rural: economy, 102–03; wages,
    101

Sahni, Dayaram, 168

Sakas, 15
Sanskrit, 22–24, 25, 26, 32, 82–83
Sanskrit College, Kolkata, 26
Sarais Act (1867), 153, 154
Sarva Shiksha Abhiyan, 132
Sassanians, 15
savings boom and Asian miracle, 127–30
Securities Exchange Bureau of India (SEBI), 152, 163
Sen, Amartya, 114
services sector, 63, 71, 74, 76–77, 134, 138
Shah Jahan, 31
Shakespeare, William, 181, 195
Sharma, Manu, 159
Shastri, Lal Bahadur, 207n[4]
Shenoy, BR, 40
Shihr, 18
ship-building technology, 20
shopping malls, 69. *See also* urbanization
Shore Nuisances (Bombay and Kolaba) Act, 1853, 153
Shourie, Arun, 151
Sikhs, 175
Silicon Valley, 65
Silk Route, 8, 10, 203
Singapore, 37, 71, 164; demographic shifts, 134
Singh, Manmohan, 48–50, 59
Singh, VP, 47
Siraj-ud-Daulah, Nawab, 176
Smith, Adam, 149
social: amenities, 169; change, 130; conflict, 160–61; infrastructure, 168; and intellectual regulation, 24; networks, 183; reforms, 2, 82; tensions, 108; values and attitudes, 84, 95, 165
socialism, 38, 76, 177

socio-economic revolution, 44, 121, 167
socio-political power structures, 180
software industry, 64, 67; revolution, 119
Solomon, 11
South China Sea, 23
South Korea, 36, 164; democracy, 180; economy, 188; literacy rate, 46; war (1950), 140, 141
Soviet Union, disintegration, 47
Special Economic Zones' (SEZs), 160–61
Spice Route, 8
Spice Trade, 203
Sri Ram College of Commerce, 108
Srivijaya kingdom, Sumatra, 11
Standard Chartered, 65
Star television, 57
state, 114 and civil society, relationship, 148; procurement systems, 104; post-liberalization, 138, 150; provision of governance, 150
State Bank of India (SBI), 61, 200
State-Carriages Act (1861), 153
State Councils for Technical Education, 116
Steel Authority of India Limited (SAIL), 86
Steel Corporation of Bengal, 198
stock market, 58, 66, 70
subsidies, 103–04
subsistence agriculture. *See* agriculture
Suharto, 180
Sumatra (Suwarnadwipa), 8, 11
Sun Microsystems, 65
Sushruta, 10
Suzuki, 44

Swatantra Party, 38, 40, 42

Tagore, Rabindranath, 31, 114, 197, 200, 201, 202; *Gitanjali*, 26–27
Taiwan, 71, 134, 164, 164, 188
Taj Mahal, 24, 31
Takshila University, 6, 110
Taliban, 62, 63, 192
Tarain, Second Battle (1192), 14
Tata group of companies, 54, 60, 144
Tata Administrative Service, 60
Tata Consultancy Services (TCS), 64
Tata Engineering and Locomotive Company (TELCO), 60
Tata Iron and Steel Company, 60
Tata, J.R.D., 40, 60
Tata Motors, 188, 190
Tata, Ratan, 60
Tata Steel, 68
Tata Tea, 68
taxation, 33, 35, 53, 89
Taxila, 11
technology, 18, 19, 20–21, 29, 31, 35, 44–45, 71, 127, 135–36, 137–38; changes, 77; shift in communications, 122; services sector, 139; stagnation, 21
Telecom Regulatory Authority of India (TRAI), 118–19
telecommunications, 73, 96, 102, 104–06, 119, 142
television, 56–57; colour transmission, 44, 56
Teresa, Mother, 212n[16]
Tetley, 68
Thadani, Vijay, 119
Thailand, 8, 9
Thyssen Krup, 68
Toyota, 68

trade union militancy, 199
traditions and rituals, 23–24
transparency, 179
transportation system, 73–74, 139
Turks, 14

Ujjaini, 11, 110
unemployment and underemployment, 78, 101
UNESCO, 56
Union Bank of Switzerland, 48
Unit Trust of India (UTI), 32
Unitech, 144
United Kingdom (British): commercial/imperial interests, 24–25; Great Reform Act (1832), 81, 173, 179; literacy, 136; middle-class, 172; Revolution (1688), 172; North American colonies, 136, 172–73
United Nations (UN), 168
United States of America (USA): terrorists' attack on WTC (9/11/2001), 62; economy, 186–87
University Grants Commission (UGC), 115–16, 119
university system, 115; reforms, 148. *See also* education
urban planning in ancient India, 5–6
urbanization, 4, 81, 165–70, 179, 183, 186. *See also* middle class, urban

Vajpayee, Atal Behari, 52, 62–63, 67
Varahmihira, 17
Velu, R., 145
Verma Committee, 113
Vespasian, Roman Emperor, 10
Vidyasagar, Ishwar Chandra, 25–26, 84, 202

Vietnam: economy, 188, 189
Vijaynagar kingdom, 16
Vivekananda, Swami, 26, 84, 197, 200
voluntary retirement schemes (VRS), 61
Volvo, 68

Walmart, 144
waste management, 169, 186
Weber, Max, 137
West Bengal: land acquisition by state for industrial unit, 160
Western: civilization, 21; knowledge, 110
Western Europe: population growth, 124–25; renaissance, 83
Westernization versus Modernization, 180–83

White Huns (Ephthalites), 110
white-collar jobs/workers, 90–92, 94, 96, 99, 101, 107, 109–10, 122, 134, 138, 177, 187, 199
William of Orange, 172
working-age population, 127, 142–43
World Bank, 199
world economy, 78; India's future place, 186–90

Y2K scare, 65
Yahya Khan, 41

Zee TV, 57
Zheng He, 20–21
Zoroastrian tradition, 11

QC
MHN
3